THE WEIMARANER

Diane Morgan

INTERPET
PUBLISHING

The Weimaraner

Project Team
Editor: Amanda Pisani
Copy Editor: Stephanie Fornino
Design: Angela Stanford
Series Design: Mada Design and Stephanie Krautheim
Series Originator: Dominique De Vito

United Kingdom Editorial Team
Hannah Turner
Nicola Parker
Claire Cullinan

First published in the United Kingdom 2008 by
Interpet Publishing
Vincent Lane
Dorking
Surrey
RH4 3YX

ISBN 978 1 84286 197 4

Copyright © 2007 by T.F.H. Publications, Inc.

Printed and bound in Indonesia

This book has been published with the intent to provide accurate and authoritative information in regard to the subject matter within. While every reasonable precaution has been taken in preparation of this book, the author and publisher expressly disclaim responsibility for any errors, omissions, or adverse effects arising from the use or application of the information contained herein. The techniques and suggestions are used at the reader's discretion and are not to be considered a substitute for veterinary care. If you suspect a medical problem consult your veterinarian.

INTERPET
PUBLISHING

www.interpet.co.uk

TABLE OF CONTENTS

HISTORY

of the Weimaraner

All breeds of dog are developed for a purpose. Border Collies herd sheep, Beagles are the ultimate rabbit specialists, and Greyhounds are the greatest racing dogs. Malamutes pull sleds, and Scottish Terriers attack vermin. All these "specialist" breeds have something in common, though. None of them were bred in Germany. You see, German breeders always approached things a bit differently.

Instead of trying to breed a single-purpose "specialist" dog, German breeders tried to create the perfect "generalist." Their chief success may have been the amazingly versatile German Shepherd Dog, but that breed lacks one vital component—it's not a hunting dog. Therefore, the Germans set out to develop an all-around hunting dog, one who could do a little of everything else, too. That's the Weimaraner.

How did they do it? And how did they come up with a dog who is not only incredibly capable but who is spectacularly beautiful as well?

EARLY HISTORY OF THE WEIMARANER

If you go back far enough into history, at least according to European dog historians (and there are such people), you will encounter the Chien Gris de Saint Louis (Grey Hounds of St. Louis), regarded as perhaps the Weimaraner's earliest recognisable ancestor. Whether these "grey hounds" were Weimaraners or "greyhounds" or neither is a considerable mystery, however.

The story states that when the French King Louis IX (Saint Louis), returned from one of the Crusades (the Seventh) in about 1248 (during which time, by the way, he was taken prisoner in Egypt), he brought with him a pack of grey deer hounds. These dogs, according to a much-cited work by Charles IX, *La Chasse Royale,* hailed from Tartary. Tartary could actually be anywhere in Europe or Asia controlled by the Tartars, who were at their height around this time. But as far as I know, they never made it to Egypt.

But who knows? This is way too long ago for anyone to figure out now. It is true that the tail of the Weimaraner makes a curious sickle-shaped curve along the last two-thirds of it—giving it a particularly Saluki-like appearance. Salukis, of course, are ancient

German breeders developed the modern Weimaraner.

sighthounds, undoubtedly bred by Tartars. Are these two breeds, far back in ancient history, related? We'll never know. Old artwork, the accuracy of which may be suspect, shows that St. Louis's "Grey Hounds" had two types of coats, both long and short. Take a look at Gobelin tapestries sometime, and see what you think. A van Dyck painting (1631) also exists that depicts a dog looking suspiciously like the modern-day version of the Weim. And a 1750 painting by Jean Baptiste Oudry, the court painter for Louis XV, an artist known for his realistic execution, shows a smooth-coated silver-grey dog named Blanche ("white" in French) stalking a game bird. Blanche has a lovely tuft on her tail.

All sources agree that the modern Weimaraner took shape in the beginning of the 19th century, the great age of dog breeding, and that German breeders can take the credit.

THE GERMANS

German foresters were looking for a breed that could both hunt and track furry game like a hound but that had more aggression against predators. In addition, they needed a pointing-type gundog who could find and retrieve birds. To top things off, the ideal dog had to be unfazed by water. For these many jobs, they sought a tireless, close worker who was easily trained but who was independent enough to do his own problem solving.

A delicate balance exists between trainability and independence; because the Germans wanted a dog bred for multiple types of game, they needed to create a temperament that was biddable yet not so dependent that the dog would be unable to think things out for himself when necessary. Because no such breed existed, the Germans decided to invent one.

Duke Karl

It's probably best to begin this part of the Weimaraner's history with the Grand Duke Karl August (1757–1828). This Grand Duke was an enlightened sort of fellow who even invited the peerless Romantic poet Goethe to Weimar, the independent court in central Germany. In 1776, he actually made Goethe a member of his privy council. "People of discernment," the Duke once remarked offhandedly, "congratulate me on possessing this man."

Duke Karl, as he was known to his pals ("August" to the rest of us), was mad about hunting in the massive forests of Thuringia. He used to ride around the countryside at breakneck speed, drank a lot, and camped out under the stars. So wild about hunting was he that he was known as "the hunter among kings and the king among hunters." He and his fellow noblemen of Weimar set about developing the breed in secret; the Weimaraner (originally the Weimar Pointer) was subsequently named after the place. According to at least one tradition, they didn't want to reveal the breed's origins to others for fear of crass imitators.

A Question of Ancestors

Duke Karl and his cohorts succeeded well enough in their secret breed development to make much of the Weimaraner's past still a puzzle. (The fact that many breeding records were destroyed during both World Wars hasn't helped matters much.) Some suggest that the Great Dane is a Weimaraner ancestor, while others lean toward the German Shorthaired Pointer. This would account for the change from a mainly hound-type dog to a mainly pointer-

The German Versatile Hunting Dog Association (GVHDA)

The GVHDA has set the standards by which versatile European hunting dogs are tested. (Not all these breeds are German, either.) Along with the Weimaraner, the GVHD breeds recognised by the Kennel Club (KC) include the Brittany, German Shorthaired Pointer, German Wirehaired Pointer and Vizsla.

The Weimaraner was developed as an all-around hunting dog.

Otto Stockmeyer, the head of the Austrian Weimaraner Club (founded in 1924) and Chief of the Department of Forestry in Grafenegg, managed to convince Prince Hans of Ratibor-Hohenlohe that the Weimaraner was so useful that the government should require every forester and hunter in the service of the government to own a member of this breed. By 1924, when the Austrian Weimaraner Club was founded, 10 of the 32 Weimaraners in Austria were owned by the Department of Forestry.

type dog seen in the Weimaraner today. Other ancestral candidates include the English Pointer, Spanish Pointer, and ultimately various sorts of Bloodhound, including the now extinct St. Hubert's Hound and the Red Schweisshund, a breed that also played a part in the development of the German Shorthaired Pointer, a dog very similar to the Weim in many respects. In fact, the first breeding entries regarding the Weimaraner appeared in the studbook of the German Shorthair Club. Another candidate is the Leithund ("Lead dog"), a hunting dog specialising in tracking large game.

Most experts do largely agree that the Weim's more recent ancestors are indigenous German hunting dogs.

Bird Dog

During the second half of the 19th century, as big game petered out in Europe, the breed was converted from a large-game hunter (including bear, boar, and deer) to a small-game hunter and bird dog. The invention of accurate firearms for hunting birds also assisted in this development. During this period, more bird-dog blood trickled into the Weimaraner line. Today, the breed hunts a variety of bird game, including pheasant, ruffed grouse, woodcock, and even ducks when it's not too cold. (The Weim's short hard coat isn't suitable for Arctic-like water.) An additional advantage of the breed for many is that it ranges fairly close to the hunter.

Today's Weimaraner hunts a variety of bird game.

At any rate, Weimaraners were given status as an independent breed in 1896 by the Reichsjaegermeister (the King's Master Hunter), who controlled such things. This "forester's dog" not only hunted and tracked wounded game, but he also assisted the game warden with bringing poachers to justice.

It's in the Eyes

Aficionados of the Spanish pointer suggest that his lighter eye colour may have been the determining factor in the same feature now seen in Weimaraners.

WEIMARANER CLUBS

On June 20, 1897, the first Weimaraner club was formed, elegantly named the "Club for the Pure Breeding of the Silver-Grey Weimaraner Vorstehhund." The purpose of the club was not to promote the breed but to protect it. Breeding guidelines were extremely strict; in fact, the total number of registered dogs was limited to 1,500. Only members of the club were allowed to breed the dogs. Litters were culled so that only the very best dogs were allowed to pass on their genes. Ludwig Beckmann, a great 19th-century authority on dogs, wrote: "There are also those of a complete silver-grey. They are described as being very attached to their master, whose voice and horn they can distinguish; they need no encouragement during hunting and are equally energetic in the cold as in the heat."

At first, the Weim was a well-kept secret, seldom seen outside his original home. However, worldwide public recognition of the breed began in 1935 during the International World Dog Exposition in Frankfurt am Main.

Another important figure in Weimaraner history was Major Robert A.D. Herber (1867–1946), the so-called Weimaraner Vater, or Weimaraner Father. He fell in love with the breed in 1915 after hunting with a dog named Held vom Artlande and was elected President of the German Weimaraner Klub (a successor to the Club for the Pure Breeding of the Silver-Grey Weimaraner Vorstehhund) in 1922.

THE GREY GHOST ARRIVES

The American figure most prominently associated with the Weimaraner is Howard Knight, a sportsman and businessman from Rhode Island. He applied for membership to the German Club, and was "accepted" only after a great struggle, promising, like every other member of the club, that he would "protect the purity of the breed." Despite Knight's avowals, the other members obviously had some doubts about Howard's intention because they sent him a pair of sterilised dogs. Knight was furious, of course, but was powerfully impressed with these dogs' hunting ability.

The Weimaraner's nickname is the "Grey Ghost."

Unwilling to surrender, Knight kept trying to obtain some breeding stock, and in 1938 managed to get several intact dogs out of Germany: litter sisters Adda and Dorle von Schwarzen Kamp; a year-old female, Aura von Gaiberg; and a male puppy, Mars aus der Wulfsreide. Aura was the first to win a championship as a bench dog, but her line became equally famous as obedience title winners. Aura's son, Ch. Grafmar's Jupiter, was the first

National Breed Clubs

The United Kingdom's version of the AKC is called the Kennel Club. However, the Kennel Club's members are individual persons. The membership of the Kennel Club is restricted to a maximum of 1,500 UK members, in addition to 50 overseas members and a small number of honorary life members. The Kennel Club promotes responsible dog ownership and works on important issues such as canine health and welfare.

The American Kennel Club (AKC), founded in 1884, is the most influential dog club in the United States. The AKC is a "club of clubs," meaning that its members are other kennel clubs, not individual people. The AKC registers purebred dogs, supervises dog shows, and is concerned with all dog-related matters, including public education and legislation. It collects and publishes the official standards for all its recognised breeds.

Weimaraner to complete all available obedience degrees. Thirty-six Grafmar dogs earned obedience titles in the next ten years. (Weims have a reputation of not excelling at obedience. However, they can do very well, if trained properly, which means respecting their intelligence and using positive reinforcement and no punishment.) Today, Knight's dogs are considered the foundation stock of modern Weimaraners. In the spirit of a true "hobby" breeder, Knight never sold any of his dogs but rather gave them as gifts to friends who he believed were worthy of the breed.

The Weimaraner Club of America (WCA) was formed in 1942 with Knight as president, and the organisation created a breed standard. The AKC formally recognised the breed later that year, and it made its debut at the Westminster Dog Show in 1943. Field trials for Weimaraners began in 1948. For the first few years of its existence, the WCA followed the practices of its German counterpart and kept strict control of breeding and selling stock. However, in 1947, Jack Denton Scott, the gundog editor of *Field and Stream* magazine, "discovered" the breed. And he publicised them to the maximum, most notably in his article "The Grey Ghost Arrives."

THE CONTEMPORARY WEIMARANER

The stately Weimaraner whom we love today is the result of conscientious breeders on the continent and, ultimately, in the United States as well.

Weims in the United Kingdom

Major R. H. Petty imported the first pair of Weimaraners into the UK in 1952, a bitch named Cobra Von Boberstrand and a dog named Bando Von Fohr. Petty had become acquainted with the breed while serving in Germany, and its hunting ability made a powerful impression on him. The breed didn't really take hold, however, until the mid-1950s, but it has rapidly gained

Dwight D.'s Dog

Whether as a trend setter or a follower, President Eisenhower owned a Weimaraner named Heidi. Heidi was a beautiful dog but fell into disgrace when she left a very bad stain on the Diplomatic Reception Room carpet; she was consequently sent back to Eisenhower's farm in Gettysburg. She probably preferred it there (more room to run). Other icons of the 1950s, including Grace Kelly, Roy Rogers, and Arthur Godfrey, also owned Weims.

popularity as a family pet, show dog, and hunting companion. The Weimaraner Club of Great Britain became affiliated with the Kennel Club in 1953. In the United Kingdom, the Weimaraner is part of the subgroup known as the "Hunt, Point, and Retrieve" breeds within the Gundog group.

Weims in the US Today

In the years immediately following World War II, demand for these silver beauties went through the roof. The 1950s, however, were a low period for Weimaraners. The beautiful Grey Ghost became a status symbol. While they triumphed in the show ring, they fell prey to increasing health and temperament problems. Unlike in Germany, no restrictions were imposed on breeders, and irresponsible and unknowledgeable people did great damage to the breed's welfare within a single decade. By 1957, these dogs ranked number 12 of 98 breeds registered by the AKC at that time. It has taken the Weim a while to recover. Puppy farms mass-produced the breed, and it became very difficult to find a good-quality show dog, hunting companion, or family pet.

In a yoyo-like response, demand dropped. By the late 1960s, new registrations for the breed fell by half, a trend that continued through the 1970s and 1980s. In recent years, most of the problems have been corrected, partly

After World War II, the Weimaraner's popularity soared.

The Wegman

No work on Weimaraners would be complete without reference to the Weims of Wegman, those ubiquitous, oft-photographed dogs of William Wegman. Wegman has won some fame as an author and a videographer for *Sesame Street*, but his name forever will be associated with the dogs whom he has immortalised. Wegman bought his first Weimaraner, Man Ray (after the artist), in the 1970s for $35.00. Man Ray soon became not merely a pet but a subject of Wegman's artistic focus. The *Village Voice* named Man Ray "Man of the Year" when the animal passed away in 1982.

Wegman wasn't interested in another dog, however, until one (subsequently named Fay Ray) was thrust upon him by an insistent breeder. Fay Ray was a terrified adolescent when Wegman got her; she was also so obsessed with a tennis ball that the artist had to keep it in the refrigerator when it was not in use. Wegman was able to use the ball to his advantage, however, and in play, Fay's true personality began to shine. Wegman added costumes and a storyline, and a star was born. Not wishing to lose the unique spark, Wegman bred Fay to a dog of famed Weimaraner breeder Virginia Anderson, and eight (highly photographed) puppies were born.

How does he get his Weims to pose? Wegman says that he doesn't bother with formal obedience but works carefully within each dog's comfort zone — he follows their natures, and the dogs always surprise him with their natural grace, humour, and charm.

While Wegman's dogs are his colleagues in photography, they are first and foremost pets who live a full and adventurous life in their New York City neighbourhood.

because of the breed's original strong gene pool and partly because it is no longer mass-produced, although Weims remain very popular and are getting more so—again.

The German Weimaraner

The Weimaraner, or Vorstehhund (Forest Hound) as he is known there, has stayed true to his roots in Germany. German Weimaraner owners have maintained his position as a beloved family pet but almost invariably use him for hunting as well. The club in Germany retains much of its power in keeping the breed strong, and as a result, the German dogs have not suffered the decline in health and character that American Weimaraners had for many years.

A Fabulous Future

The future of this noble breed is bright. Improved breeding practices, a better understanding of genetics, and a public that is more aware ensure that the glorious Grey Ghost will continue to possess the soul of his master for many generations to come.

Chapter 2

CHARACTERISTICS

of the Weimaraner

D espite his nickname, the Grey Ghost, there's nothing wraithlike about the Weimaraner, except maybe his haunting beauty (and slightly spooky gaze). On the contrary, this breed is so vibrantly alive that it's almost overwhelming. In fact, for some people it *is* overwhelming. Welcome to Weim World. Do you think that you can possess the Grey Ghost? No—you will be possessed by him—in more ways than one.

THE WEIMARANER STANDARD

The breed standard describes the most desirable qualities—regarding both physical attributes and temperament—of the Weimaraner.

General Appearance

He should be a medium-sized grey dog, with fine aristocratic features. He should show grace, speed, stamina, alertness and balance. His build ("conformation") should indicate that he can work with great speed and endurance in the field. This is a sturdy, powerful-looking dog.

Height

Height at the withers: dogs, 24 to 27 inches (61 to 69 cm); bitches, 22 to 25 inches (56 to 64 cm). Dogs measuring less than 24 inches (61 cm) or more than 28 inches (71 cm), and bitches measuring less than 22 inches (56 cm) or more than 26 inches (66 cm) shall be disqualified. The standard doesn't mention weight, but a Weimaraner in good shape should weigh between 50 and 70 pounds (22.7 and 31.8 kg). Heavy dogs are less effective than leaner dogs at working in the field.

Head

The head should be aristocratic looking and medium long, with moderate stop (the point at which the foreface meets the back part of the skull) and the head should have a slight median line extending back over the forehead. He should have a rather prominent occipital bone (the back part of the skull) and the temples should be well set back, beginning at the back of the eye sockets. The measurement from the tip of the nose to the stop should equal that from the stop to the occipital bone. The flews (the part of the upper lip that hangs down) should enclose a very strong jaw and be reasonably deep. The neck should be moderately long and have a clean cut look. And the expression is shown to be with intelligence. The eyes should be amber, grey, or blue-grey, set well enough apart to indicate a good disposition and intelligence. When dilated under excitement, the eyes can sometimes appear almost black. Puppies often have blue eyes.

The Weimaraner's head looks aristocratic.

The teeth strong, even and well-set, well developed and proportionate to the jaw with correct scissors bite; the upper teeth protruding slightly over the lower teeth. The nose should be grey, but the lips and gums should be shades of pink flesh colour.

Body

"Imposing" is the best word to describe the Weim's body. This dog is an athlete, and it should show in his taut, well-muscled body.

Coat and Colour

The correct coat is short, smooth, and sleek. The proper colour is solid and silver-grey, usually blending to lighter shades on the head and ears. A small white marking on the chest is permitted but will be penalised on any other portion of the body. White spots resulting from injury should not be penalised." These are called "honorable scars" and are always assumed to have been incurred while on the hunt—even if what really happened was a nip from a Chihuahua. With Weimaraners, though, sometimes it's the same thing.

The Blue Weimaraner

So-called "blue" Weimaraners may not compete in conformation events. They are relatively rare in the UK, but more popular in the US and are recognised as a purebred by the AKC. While the KC considers a blue or black coat a fault, these colours, especially the blue, have their backers. There are some breeders who particularly like this colour and are actually breeding to enhance it. Blue Weimaraners are eligible to compete in field trials, obedience, and in fact any sanctioned KC event except conformation.

In the mid-20th century, the members of the Weimaraner Club of America (WCA) simply decided that they did not want dogs with a "blue" coat. They petitioned the AKC to disqualify such blue coats, and while the AKC did not agree, in the 1953 revision of the standard, both blue coats and long coats were clumped together as "very serious faults." The standard read: "Any long-haired coat or coat darker than mouse-grey to silver-grey is considered a most undesirable recessive trait." Blue is not a "recessive" trait, but no matter. At any rate, the standard distinctly overturned the 1944 standard that clearly stated that acceptable Weimaraner colour could be "grey (silver, bright, dark, yellow); the dark grey may be either ash or *blue* ..." (my emphasis). However, by the 1960s, there was a stronger and stronger push to disqualify blue dogs from the show ring. Opponents to the blue colour came close in 1965, when longhairs were disqualified, but blues managed to hang in until 1972, when the present standard was adopted. Blues (and blacks) are now finally officially disqualified, although plenty of people like the colour.

The Long-Haired Weimaraner

Reports of long-haired Weimaraners in litters from short-haired parents began appearing toward the end of the 19th century, and they were duly entered in dog shows, just like their short-haired cousins. However, they have never been common in the show ring. Rather oddly, both the sleek, very short coat of the more familiar

What Is a Standard?

The standard is a written picture of the ideal dog. No photograph is ever used because no real dog can be ideal. The ideal can be created only in the imagination of every owner. The written standard is intended to guide that imagination. This is the guideline that a dog show judge uses to select the best Weimaraner in a conformation class. Your pet Weimaraner may have several "faults" that do not disqualify him from being a great pet. In fact, you can sometimes get a dog with excellent bloodlines but who has a minor flaw, like too big a white spot on the chest, that would make him a poor show prospect, even if his other features are good.

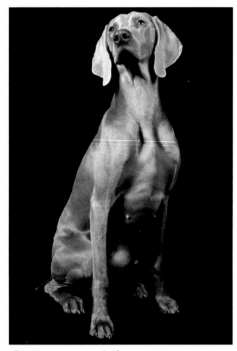

The Weim comes in shades of mouse-grey to silver-grey.

No Need for Clairol!

People still cannot agree on the source of the Weimaraner's colour. Some suggest that it may be the result of some ancient albinism present in old German pointing dogs. Others think that the colour comes from the German hound, the Brachen, and point to a crossing between a regular German pointer and a "yellow pointer" by Grand Duke Karl August of Weimar.

Weim and the long-haired coat are fairly recent developments, and it's probable that they both antedate the "stockhaarig" coat, the medium-type coat such as you'd find on today's Beagle. This "stockhaarig" coat type is not accepted in Germany, although German breeders believe that an occasional cross of a longhair with a *stockhaarig* produces a finer coat in the descendants. If they wish to add a *stockhaairg* dog to their breeding programme, they must apply for permission.

Long hair in the Weim is produced by an autosomal recessive gene. This means that when carriers are mated, the odds are that the puppies will be 25 percent longhairs, 25 percent short-haired noncarriers, and 50 percent short-haired carriers of the long-haired trait. Individual litters vary considerably, however. About a quarter of the Weimaraners born in Germany today have long hair. Although earlier versions of the long-haired Weim carried their tail high over their backs, today a lower tail carriage is more commonly seen.

The United States is the *only* country in which the long-haired Weim is not recognised! However, although not allowed by the AKC standard, long-haired Weimaraners do exist and were recognised in Germany in 1935. While the coat is usually smooth and silky, there are also hard- and rough-coated varieties, as well as the "normal" long-haired variety. The adult long-haired Weimaraner coat may be flat with feathering (either sparse or luxuriant), or it may be long all over. In any case, it gets longer and thicker during cold weather. It can be straight or slightly wavy. Long-haired Weim puppies have a kind of woolly coat.

In Germany today, there are variances in the long-haired coat in regard to length, texture, and amount of undercoat. In temperament, however, the long-haired Weimaraner is very similar to that of the short-haired version—devoted to his owner and eager to hunt. Before 1935, German breeders attempted to eliminate the long-haired trait, but as they did, they started running into other undesirable traits in shorthairs, such as a sparse, brittle coat over-sensitive skin and thyroid problems. German breeders, therefore, decided that eliminating the long-haired variety could, in the long run, be detrimental to the breed as a whole. Some people strongly suspect that the same is also true in the United States.

Because Germany is the home of the Weimaraner, the Fédération Cynologique Internationale (FCI), the organisation which the German Kennel Club (VDH) is associated, also accepts the long-haired variety. Like the KC, the FCI is a registry and maintains a studbook and other records at its headquarters in Belgium. According to FCI rules, the parent club in each breed's *native* country is recognised as the international breed club, and its

Long-haired Weimaraners exist, but are not as common as the short-haired variety.

standard is the official international standard. Thus, the German standard, not the KC one, is the Weim's "official international standard," and longhairs are accepted.

Most Weim experts believe that long hair in Weims is a recessive gene ultimately derived from the Spanish Pointer (*Perdiguero de Navarro*), not from setter-like bird dogs. The Spanish breed, almost destroyed during World War II, has both short-haired and long-haired varieties. Some dog historians think that the long-haired trait was simply hidden for generations and appeared suddenly when two carriers were mated.

Aficionados of the long-haired coat believe that it's an asset for hunting dogs because the coarse topcoat repels water, while the softer undercoat insulates against the cold. Of course, these dogs do require more grooming than the short-coated variety.

While long hair is a disqualifying fault for conformation in the United States, a long-haired Weim is eligible to be registered with the AKC if both its parents are registered. He also can compete in all sanctioned AKC events except for conformation.

Presently, a great fuss exists in the Weimaraner community about the wisdom of "requalifying" longhairs. Because the long hair is a true recessive trait, people who favour shorthairs are truly troubled about how to manage their lines to keep out the increasingly pervasive long-haired gene. Perhaps when more about the genetic heritage of Weimaraners is understood, those on either side of the issue can be satisfied. In an ideal world, long-haired Weims should be available to those who want them, while breeders of short-haired Weims should be able to produce the kind of dogs that they desire without having to worry about long-haired puppies suddenly showing up out of nowhere.

Legs

The legs are long and muscular. The forelegs should be straight.

Feet and Nails

These athletic dogs can be good swimmers.

The round feet should be firm and compact, webbed. Toes should be well arched with the pads closed and thick. The nails should be short and grey or amber in colour. The dewclaws should be removed. This is for the dog's own protection. Dewclaws are quite useless and can get caught on things. With their webbed feet, Weimaraners are good swimmers. They are not, however, "natural" swimmers, and so they may have to be taught to swim.

Tail

Whilst docking of the tail used to be allowed in the UK, it is now banned and the tail should be in proportion to the body reaching down to the hocks and thinning towards the tip. It may be raised and curled over the back when your Weimaraner is excited, but would normally be carried below the level of the back and should have good hair coverage.

Docking

This is as good a place as any to mention the tail docking debate, which is a very hot potato in the United Kingdom and becoming increasingly so in the United States, with several welfare and veterinary groups against, many breed clubs for, and plenty of other people in the middle.

Proponents of tail docking say that the procedure is relatively painless, improves the aesthetics of the breed, is traditional, and cuts down on injuries to hunting dogs and constant tail waggers. They maintain that docked dogs are happy, well-adjusted animals. They also believe that the nervous system is so undeveloped at the age that docking is done that the puppies feel minimal pain. (I must disagree. I have been present at tail dockings. The puppies whimper and cry and bleed, and they are obviously in pain.)

Opponents believe the procedure to be unnatural and painful. They contend, moreover, that it puts dogs at a serious disadvantage in communicating with other dogs and people. (This last is perhaps less true with the Weimaraner, who is given a good 6 inches [15.2 cm] of tail to work with, than it is of other docked breeds.) The tail, after all, is there for a reason. It helps the dog balance and is really useful for a running, turning dog. During a hard turn, a dog throws the front part of his body in its intended direction. The back then curves, but the forward velocity is such that the hindquarters tend to continue in the first, original direction. The tail keeps the dog's rear end from swinging too widely, which could slow him down or even force him to topple over. Opponents also report that adverse side effects of docking can include infection, nerve damage, self-mutilation, faecal incontinence, and perineal hernias.

Gait

The gait should be effortless and should indicate smooth coordination. When seen from the rear, the hind feet should be

Shedding

Just because Weimaraners have a short coat doesn't mean that they don't shed. They do, and they can shed a lot. The hair seems to stick to everything.

His Big Bark

The standard doesn't say anything about this, but the bark of a Weimaraner, in my view, is important. It should be big, deep, and authoritative—something that might impress a stranger. Weims can be wary of people they don't know and so make excellent watchdogs. Some Weims tend to be nuisance barkers if not correctly managed.

parallel to the front feet. When viewed from the side, the topline should remain strong and level.

Temperament

The temperament of the Weimaraner should be friendly, fearless, alert, and obedient. This dog is extremely loyal to his family and is protective although never aggressive. Although the breed is a hunter, its primary love is its human—not the chase. This is not a breed that does well kept in a kennel. Your Weim requires human companionship. Be aware that separation anxiety is very prominent in this breed.

LIVING WITH A WEIM

The Weimaraner is a powerful, strong-willed animal originally bred to hunt boar and bear. He requires an owner who can take charge and be a good leader. Weak, wishy-washy people are poor Weim owners.

A properly socialised Weimaraner is a joy to have around; he is friendly and safe. However, unsocialised dogs can be suspicious of strangers, skittish, or even aggressive.

Exercise Needs

Don't expect your Weim to glide silently through the house like a dim shadow. He is quicksilver on four legs. There are few if any breeds of dog that require more exercise to keep fit and happy. Sufficient exercise for the Weimaraner is not a saunter around the

There are few if any breeds of dog that require more exercise to keep fit and happy.

block or even a 2-mile (3.2-m) jog. This dog needs to run hard and often. If you enjoy a sedentary lifestyle, you may have to hire not a dog walker but a dog runner to keep your Weim content. If your highly energetic dog doesn't receive an adequate outlet for his relentless energy, he'll create his own—and you may not like the results. Some Weimaraner owners have gone so far as to characterise the resultant destruction of a sofa or even an entire room as "spiteful," but it's fairer to say that the Weim has an acute sense of what he needs in the way of entertainment and stimulation. In the wrong home, this elegant and aristocrat canine will morph beyond ghosthood into a barking, digging, destructive demon.

The intense energy of the young Weimaraner also may make him unsuited to a home with small children or frail elderly people who can be bowled over by this spinning, jumping, bouncy creature.

Work Out With Your Weim

You should exercise your Weim daily unless the weather is dangerous or he has a medical problem that limits his activity.

Prey Drive

Developed as an all-around hunting dog, the Weimaraner has a strong prey drive. This can translate into aggression against other animals, and in the male, aggression against other male dogs. They are great chasers of bicyclists, cats, joggers, and even cars. With some individuals, everything that runs—from guinea pigs to deer—could be in peril. In a very few cases, a running child, especially one who is crying or screaming, could be a trigger. Not every single Weimaraner has a prey drive of such intensity, but many do. This is an instinct that cannot be "trained out" of Weimaraners who have it. It only can be managed.

THOSE DOGGY SENSES

While you and your Weimaraner have the same basic sensory equipment, the strength of your senses and how you prioritise them may differ.

Smell

Unless you're *really* into aromatherapy, sense of smell is a much more critical component in the life of your Weimaraner than it is in you. It gives him essential information about the environment and other dogs—not just physical information but also psychological insight into that dog's state of mind. It tells him where you've been when you have been so rude as to leave him alone for a

Weims and Kids

Weimaraners love children, especially their "own." They may be too energetic for little ones, though, unless carefully supervised.

couple hours. Human beings rely upon a dog's supernose to track lost kids, locate skiers buried in snow, find bombs, and perhaps even detect cancer. A canine's success at these tasks is due to the presence of more than 200 million scent receptors located in his nasal folds. (Humans have only about 5 million.)

Sight

Dogs are not the colour-blind, dim-sighted creatures we once supposed them to be. They can distinguish between certain colours,

Older children and Weims can get along very well if taught to respect each other.

although these hues probably appear duller to them than they do to us. They cannot distinguish between red, orange, yellow, or green, but they can distinguish various shades of blue and grey better than humans can. They see better than humans do at night, and they pick up movement better than humans can. They have better peripheral vision, too.

Hearing

A dog's hearing is far more acute than a human's hearing. Dogs can hear sounds from farther away, and their hearing extends to a greater range of frequency. In addition, the mobility of their ears allows them to quickly find the source of a sound. And Weimaraners, with their lop ears, can hear just as well as Siberian Huskies, who have erect ones.

Touch

Touch is the mother sense. Before a puppy can see or hear, he can feel. And like a human's body, your Weimaraner's entire body is covered with delicate nerve endings. Because he has such a close coat, he is probably more sensitive to touch than a heavily coated Samoyed. His whiskers also are extremely sensitive, even capable of detecting airflow.

Taste

Dogs have taste buds, but not nearly as many as humans do—and some of them are located in the throat, so they can literally taste their food as they gobble it down. Most of the rest of the taste buds are found at the tip of the tongue. Dogs do have the same sorts of taste buds that humans do—sweet, sour, bitter, and salty—but no one knows how they respond to them.

The Sixth Sense

This is where the ghostly part returns. We don't know for certain whether dogs have a sixth sense, but they appear to be able to detect changes in the earth's magnetic field as well as changes in barometric pressure. During the catastrophic 2004 Indian Ocean earthquake and subsequent tsunami, unchained dogs knew something was up long before their masters did, and they headed for high ground.

PREPARING
for Your Weimaraner

Why a Weim? The answer is obvious, isn't it? No other breed has the Weimaraner's combination of line, elegance, fluidity, and power. A Weimaraner is music in motion. But remember, the Weimaraner is no waltzer. He's swing and jitterbug and krumping all rolled into one. Unless you are absolutely committed to providing this dog with the furious exercise that he needs every day, you are barking up the wrong breed. And because they are so people-oriented, Weims are right only for folks who spend a lot of time at home. Count up how many hours you can spend at home with your dog a week. If you work 40 hours or more a week and have an active social or weekend life that doesn't include dogs, you'll have a pretty unhappy Weim on your hands. And unless you have a strong personality that can handle a demanding and dominant dog, look elsewhere.

But if you love exercise and dog-related activities, if you're home a lot and are a strong leader, a Weim is your perfect match. Get ready!

PUPPY OR ADULT?

Weimaraners come in two "varieties:" immature (puppy) and mature (dog). All dogs start as puppies,

Reality Check

The average Weim is nothing like the neurotic Beatrice in the hit movie *Best in Show*. The film does point out the fact that even the best-bred dog can get a little crazy when paired with the wrong owners. The dog who played the part, by the way, is Canadian Champion Arokat's Echobar Take Me Dancing, who is anything but neurotic. She is a therapy dog, as well as a top show dog.

You'll have to decide if you want a puppy or an adult.

and all puppies turn into dogs. Most people, especially most first-time dog owners, want a puppy. Puppies are wonderful! They are warm, cuddly, and absolutely irresistible. Choosing a puppy has several advantages. You get to train the dog right from the start, and you don't have to deal with the training mistakes of former owners. If you get your pup from a good breeder, you'll probably have a healthy and psychologically sound dog. However, puppies aren't for everyone. Remember that your precious 5-pound (2.3 kg) puppy will turn into 70 fast-moving pounds (31.8 kg) in less than a year.

While puppies are charming and undeniably cute, there are many reasons to consider getting an older dog. One obvious reason is, well, looks. A puppy, even from a reputable breeder, is always something of an unknown quantity. An adult dog, on the other hand, is there in all his size and glory. Older dogs are usually housetrained, and they have finished with the disastrous chewing stage. And despite the old adage, old dogs *can* learn, and they learn quickly. In fact, they have a longer attention span and are less likely to be distracted than puppies. Additionally, older dogs are often well socialised and understand how to get along with others—something that many puppies still have to experience. Older dogs are loving and grateful to have a good home. They need less supervision than puppies do, and they are instantly ready to join you in long walks and other grown-up activities. And they won't keep you awake all night crying for their mothers.

Of course, there's a downside to everything. Many older dogs are given up because of temperament or training problems, so be sure that you know the whole story before you decide to adopt an older dog.

MALE OR FEMALE?

The gender of the dog for you is a matter of personal preference. If you already have a dog, it's often wise to choose a second dog of the opposite sex, but there's no hard and fast rule about this. There also isn't any real character difference between male and female dogs. Choose the dog who most appeals to you, then worry about the sex. Unless you are showing your Weim, you should have him neutered.

FINDING THAT SPECIAL WEIMARANER

Getting the right dog for you and your family is a little more complicated than simply pulling out your credit card. If you want a dog to show in the ring, you'll definitely want to get your Weim from a breeder. Be prepared to spend a nice sum of money. If you don't plan to show your dog, there are several avenues to explore.

Buying a Weim

If your heart is irretrievably set on a puppy, your best bet is a reputable breeder. The breeder will ask you many questions. Her main interest is not making money (and in spite of how much the dog may cost you, you'd be surprised to learn how little good breeders make on selling a dog) but improving the breed and finding the right homes for her puppies. She may ask you questions about your lifestyle, your expectations, and your knowledge of the breed. The key is to be completely honest with the breeder about your intentions. If you are seriously interested in field trials or hunting, say so. If your interests lie more toward a companion or show dog, tell her that. Breeders are not mind readers, and they can help you make appropriate choices only if you give them enough information to allow them to do so.

Healthy puppies look clean with shiny coats, bright eyes, and no bare patches or discharge from eyes, nose, ears, or rear.

Be sure to ask the breeder some questions, and come prepared with a list. Your questions might include:

- What is the goal of breeding this litter?
- What events have the parents competed in, and what titles have they earned?
- Is there a photograph of the sire available if the sire is not on the premises?
- What health clearances do the parents and grandparents have? (You should be especially interested in hip and elbow dysplasia, which are common in Weimaraners.)
- How often has she seen bloat (a deadly gastric problem) in her line?

A Shelter Dog Bonus

Nearly all shelters and rescue organisations require their dogs to be neutered before they are released. Not only is this ethical, but it's a real money saver for you.

- Have the puppies visited the vet for their first health check?
- What health guarantees come with the puppy?

If the breeder can't answer these questions to your satisfaction, look elsewhere.

If you're not planning to show and you are dealing with a breeder who specialises in conformation, explain that you are looking for a "pet-quality" Weimaraner. This doesn't mean that there will be anything at all wrong with the puppy. It just means that in the breeder's opinion, the puppy will not achieve a championship in the show ring. A few unimportant factors may limit a dog's "show worthiness" but have no effect on his ability to make a great companion for you and your family.

Rescue Organisations and Shelters

Adopting a dog from a shelter or rescue makes a real, tangible difference in more lives than you can imagine. First of all, every shelter, every pound, and every rescue group in the country is full to capacity. Every day, thousands of dogs are put to sleep—not because they are ill or vicious—but because there is simply no more room for them. Few dogs who go to the shelter will find homes, and many are euthanised. Rescue groups have better success in placing dogs, but most do not have the resources to take in large numbers of dogs. When you accept a shelter/rescue dog into your home, you are making room for another dog who may now have a chance at life. You've saved two dogs!

Dogs are given up to rescues and shelters for various reasons. Sometimes a dog's former owner dies. Sometimes a dog is found as a stray or collected because of owner abuse. Sometimes people decide they no longer want their dog for a variety of reasons. Just because a dog has been put in a rescue or shelter does not necessarily mean that you can adopt one for free, however. Rescue groups depend on donations and backbreaking fundraisers. Many of the dogs they receive require extensive medical care, frequently because of mistreatment or neglect.

Although they have been "dumped," rescue and shelter dogs are not rubbish. Some even shine in competition! Many adopted dogs have gone on to earn performance titles or excel at therapy work. And while it's true that many adopted dogs come with "baggage," kind treatment and patience usually work wonders. Dogs are much more flexible than people, and with loving care, most manage to forget their gloomy pasts.

The difference you'll make in your new dog's life will be immeasurable. You may be providing your rescue Weim's first toy, bed, and love. You may be taking him for his first walk, his first romp, his first game of catch. You may be giving him the first kind words he's ever heard. However, the biggest difference will be in your own life. The feeling of having saved a life will enhance and enrich your own. The love you get from a previously unloved and unwanted dog easily matches any facile puppy devotion.

Like the pickiest of breeders, rescue organisations are also concerned that your new dog will fit with your lifestyle and will try to place a dog whose characteristics suit your needs.

PUPPY PROOFING

Your Weimaraner deserves a safe and friendly environment. These dogs crave companionship, and if they are not socialised and entertained, they will create havoc out of their environment. These highly intelligent dogs can and will find a way to open any door or gate. Weims can climb over fences, dig under them, and go through

You may find the Weim of your dreams at a rescue or shelter.

Taking Love to Another Level

There is something even more important that you can do for a rescue organisation than adopting from one. Consider becoming a foster parent! Foster parents take in and care for needy dogs under the auspices of the organisation. Every group is different, but most will reimburse you for your veterinary bills and food costs. Some pay for professional training for the dog. Most have mentors to whom you can turn for help.

To be a good foster parent, you should be willing to exercise and play with the Weim on a daily basis, have plenty of patience. (Many of these dogs have just been through traumatic experiences and need you to help to make them whole again.) In some cases, you may have to work on housetraining or other behavioural concerns. You also will have to be able to follow the procedures of the organisation you work with.

The hardest part about being a foster parent is giving up the dog when his permanent new family enters the picture. Many fosters are tempted to adopt the dog themselves, feeling perhaps that no one else could ever love the dog as much as they did. But having the courage to give up the Weim when the time is right makes room in the home for a new needy dog—and that's doing something that really makes a difference.

them (and that includes so-called "invisible" or electric fences). This doesn't mean that they will do this as a matter of course—it means they *can* do these things if left alone for long periods without adequate stimulation. In all honesty, it is much tougher to keep a Weim out of trouble than, say, a Bulldog.

The Kitchen

Household cleaning solutions are one of the five most common causes of pet poisoning in the home. Soaps, detergents, shampoos, alcohols, petroleum distillates, and acids can cause nausea, vomiting, diarrhoea, and chemical burns, leading to organ damage. If you're not accustomed to keeping these items out of your dog's reach, now is a good time to start.

The Bathroom

The big danger in the bathroom is drugs, both prescription and over-the-counter. These can be lethal to a dog. And remember, a childproof cap is not a dogproof cap. Dogs simply chew the cap off. It takes a Weimaraner about three seconds to do this if he is feeling lazy.

Safe Medicine Storage

All drugs always should be placed out of reach of dogs and children.

The Garage

The most dangerous part of your house is undoubtedly the garage, and the items in this section are just a sampling of the dangers that may be lurking there. Keep your Weim away from it. Also, retain all products in their original containers, and make sure that the label is intact and readable before using them.

Noxious items found there include:

Antifreeze

Antifreeze is a deadly poison that, when metabolised and transported to the kidneys, forms insoluble calcium oxalate crystals that will kill your dog. A few teaspoons are lethal. Unfortunately, dogs like the sweet taste of the stuff. While antifreeze containing propylene glycol is less dangerous than the ethylene glycol most commonly used, it's all bad. If you drain your antifreeze, do not leave it in an open container because dogs are attracted by its sweet taste. Keep any containers that have or have had antifreeze in them away from dogs, who may be tempted to chew them.

Before You Fertilize

Remove water dishes, food bowls, and your Weim from the garden before applying lawn care products.

Deck Washes

Deck washes may contain alkaline corrosives that cause chemical burns.

Fertilizers

These can cause vomiting and gastric irritation. Some of the so-called systemic fertilizers (commonly used around roses) are very deadly.

Herbicides

While safe when used as directed, herbicides can cause vomiting and diarrhoea if a dog gets into them. A few brands even contain arsenic!

Puppy proof your home before your Weim arrives.

If Your Dog Is Poisoned

If you suspect that your dog has been poisoned, contact your veterinarian immediately. Have the following information ready:

- name of the substance or product
- amount that was absorbed, ingested, or inhaled
- when you think the poisoning occurred
- weight of your dog
- signs of poisoning: vomiting, tremors, excessive salivation, colour of gums, heart and breathing rates, and if practical, body temperature

Paint Thinners

Paint thinners can cause inflammation to the lungs if inhaled.

Pesticides

Pesticides are not usually harmful when applied according to directions. The big danger comes from concentrated products, especially when the products are overused or improperly stored. Insecticides are most dangerous because they have a higher degree of toxicity than other pesticides.

Rat and Mouse Poison

Many rodenticides can cause uncontrolled haemorrhage, although other types exist that are even more lethal to your dog. If you absolutely must use a rodenticide, choose the traditional anticoagulant kind, which, while lethal, does have an antidote (injections of vitamin K) if you get your dog to the vet fast enough. Unfortunately, anticoagulant rodenticide produces no symptoms in your dog for several days, even though he could be slowly bleeding to death internally. There is no antidote for some other kinds of rodenticides.

Road Salt and De-Icers

If your dog eats these items, they can cause vomiting and diarrhoea. Some kinds can build up, penetrate the brain, and cause a host of neurological problems. Even if your Weim gets them on his paws, they can cause skin irritation.

Snail and Slug Bait

Snail and slug bait products contain metaldehyde, which can

34

cause seizures and coma in dogs. Signs of poisoning occur within 30 minutes of ingestion. Pets who ingest even tiny amounts of metaldehyde must be treated immediately by a veterinarian. (Some of this stuff is even coated in molasses and is shaped like dog food, which doesn't help.) Consider using a nontoxic form of snail and slug bait, or use traps baited with beer or "slug dough," a mixture of molasses, cornmeal, flour, water, and yeast, to attract pests.

Fences

Your Weim needs a safe, secure, fenced garden. Your best bet is a standard wood and wire or chain link fence at least 5 feet (1.5 m) high.

The Lawn

The most serious dangers to dogs presented by your lawn are the products that you may coat it with. Lawn care products fall into three categories: fertilizers, insecticides, and herbicides. As mentioned earlier, insecticides tend to be the most toxic. However, most products are safe enough if you read the label and follow the directions, which generally advise keeping pets away from freshly applied areas. A treated lawn should be completely dry after waiting the maximum

Check your for dangerous objects and poisonous plants. (Luckily, these pansies are safe.

Mulch Mess

One popular new type of mulch uses cocoa bean hulls. Dogs find this stuff very attractive, but it is extremely dangerous. First, cocoa bean hulls are full of theobromine, which is toxic to dogs in and of itself. Second, devouring large amounts of mulch is just a gastrointestinal disaster on so many levels. Don't use this stuff.

period recommended on the label. To be extra safe, water the lawn and let it dry again after application. If you use dry, granular pesticides, wait until the dust settles before letting your dog on it.

If your Weim gets out and you spot him rolling in the lawn too soon, wash him off with a mild shampoo and check with your vet. Signs of poisoning with lawn care products include stumbling, salivating, vomiting, or having seizures. If you see these, call your vet immediately. Don't forget to have the product in hand so that you can tell the veterinarian what chemical your pet may have been exposed to. You also may contact them for information about less toxic lawn care products.

The Pool

Weims can be good swimmers, but that doesn't mean that the pool is safe for an unsupervised dog. If you have a pool, you should teach your dog where the pool stairs are and make sure that he can swim. A see-through pool barrier is a good way to keep your dog and pool separated. The gate should be self-closing and self-locking. You even can buy a floating pool alarm that will go off when the surface of the pool is disturbed.

To get your dog accustomed to the pool, go into the shallow end and keep him afloat by holding him beneath the pelvis. Make sure that his head is above water and his hindquarters are up. It may take some time before your dog feels comfortable in the water. Never throw a dog into the pool; he may panic and not be able to climb the slick sides to get out. Also, he can tear your vinyl liner while trying. Be patient. Dogs are natural swimmers; they just need to develop the skill.

Watch your older dog carefully around the pool; as dogs age, even formerly great swimmers lose the strength in their limbs to swim well. And for dogs of all ages, even hanging around the edge of pool can be a bad idea. It's usually much hotter because it's located in direct sunlight. Heatstroke is a very real possibility. By the way, a covered pool can be even more dangerous than an open one. Dogs can fall through or get through most pool covers and then drown because they can't get back out.

EQUIPMENT

Before bringing a dog into your life, be prepared to have the house stocked with the stuff you'll need—doggy dishes, a bed, and the like. You'll want to make your new best friend feel right at home.

Bed

Your dog should have a comfortable place of his own in which to sleep. Because puppies don't mind sleeping anywhere (and are prone to chew), you might just want to fold up some old blankets for a temporary bed. (Your dog will probably chew and rip them up anyway.) When he gets over his major chewing stage, buy him a sturdy bed of his own. Many are completely washable; others have washable covers.

Post-Pool Rinse

If your pool is heavily chlorinated, you may want to rinse your dog off (including his eyes) afterward. Don't panic if he drinks the water, though. It won't hurt him.

Collar

A collar is essential for your dog. It will hold his ID tags and provide a quick and convenient handle when you need to grab him quickly. And they come in such an array of charming colours and styles that you will easily find one to your taste.

Flat Collars

Most well-trained dogs do best on a simple flat collar. These come in a variety of materials, including leather, nylon, and cotton web. (You can get simple cotton cloth also, but web is stronger.) Nylon usually outlasts cotton, but it can be irritating to sensitive skin, especially the cheaper kinds. Polypropylene collars, which are narrow and rolled, combine many of the good qualities of nylon and cotton; they are as sturdy as the former and as soft as the latter. However, a dog who tends to pull can injure his trachea on such a narrow collar. A good-quality leather collar is hard to beat, but cheaper varieties smell bad and wear through easily. Some leather collars are coloured with an awful dye that bleeds into the dog's fur as well. Avoid these.

You also can select a buckle collar or an easy-snap fastener collar. Some very large dogs can pop a snap fastener with a concerted lunge, though, so your best bet may be a sturdy buckle collar.

Choke, Prong, and Electric Collars

Choke, prong, and electric collars are lumped together here because they are a bad idea for almost everyone. A case can be made that each has a place if used correctly by a skilled trainer,

A flat collar is best for your Weim, and an ID that is punched into the collar like this is very secure.

but very few people are skilled trainers. Even proponents of choke collars admit that most people do not use them correctly; in fact, most people do not even put them on correctly. Because of the likelihood of improper use (with the dog suffering as a result), I suggest that they not be used at all.

Choke collars and prong collars can damage a dog's trachea if not used properly. It is possible to actually kill a dog with one. And while prong collar enthusiasts insist that the prongs do not really hurt a dog because the correction is distributed evenly around the neck, that's not true. Of course prong collars hurt. That's the whole purpose of them. Try one on yourself if you don't believe me.

Shock collars are the worst of the lot. Even though they can be tuned down to give only a mild buzz, their potential for abuse is so high that I cannot recommend them. They simply make the statement that the owner is too inept to train her dog properly.

Head Halters

One of the latest trends in training gear is head halters; proponents maintain that they're humane and safe. They also claim that they're easy to use; however, they're not easy to put on! Head halters are similar to those used for horses and work on the simple principle that if you control the dog's head, you control the whole dog. They require less physical force than a conventional collar and can't choke the dog like a choke collar. People who have trouble handling their Weim on regular collars often resort to head halters.

Head halters cannot be worn without human supervision, and because tags should be on your dog at all times, they can only be an addition to, not a replacement of, a regular collar.

I should warn you that your Weim will not like the head halter when you first put it on him. He may shake or rub his head, try to run away, rear up, or perform a host of other behaviours that tell you in no uncertain terms what he thinks of it. Usually, this is a brief revolt, and most dogs settle down within a few minutes. It usually helps to move the dog very briskly along for the first adventure with the head halter. The head halter comes with training instructions.

Front-Loop Harness

I have found an alternative to the head halter—the front-loop harness. This harness is easy to use, more dog friendly, and I think more effective. It is similar to a regular harness except that the lead loop is in the front, low on the chest. You lead your dog easily and comfortably. I have seen this harness work on dogs where absolutely nothing else would—and the dogs love it!

Crate

Having a crate will help make life with your Weim easier. It helps with housetraining, is essential for travel, and can be lifesaver if you need to confine your dog because of illness or injury. Many dogs seem to enjoy their crates, treating them like a den. Others detest them and have to be bribed to get them into one. The different attitudes depend largely on their early experiences with this plastic or wire box. Dogs who are isolated in crates for long periods every day grow to hate them and can even develop a post-traumatic barrier anxiety as a result. Dogs who have had positive experiences with crates regard them as places of security.

Crate Styles

You have a wide choice of styles and materials from which to choose. Many professional handlers use aluminum crates. They

A Dog's Attitude Toward His Crate

Tougher, more dominant dogs tend to develop the strongest attitudes about crates. Some hate them and refuse to enter them. Others take possession of them and will not allow their owners to coax them out.

are sturdy, rust-free, and lightweight, a big plus when dealing with more than one dog. (In fact, some of these crates divide into compartments for this purpose.) Some are airline approved. They have a pull-out floor for easy cleaning, and many are collapsible. The big drawback to these crates is that they tend to be costly. You can get a much cheaper collapsible plastic crate; some models come with carrying straps and storage bags. Most of these crates are designed for smaller dogs, however.

Heavy-duty plastic or fibreglass crates are required for many airlines. They are very strong, even for serious diggers and chewers. Most have doors made of metal grating, and they can be heavy and difficult to take apart. Some dogs prefer their den-like darkness, but the limited visibility and venting can make them too hot in some environments. Cost varies with size and quality.

For sheer charm, a handsome lightweight wicker or wicker-like (usually a plastic resin) basket is unbeatable. However, true wicker will absorb every smell deposited on it and it can be chewed

A crate makes travelling easy and safe.

through; imitations are somewhat tougher.

Wire crates have lots of ventilation and visibility. They are easy to clean, and the new ones fold up and transport easily. Some dogs like their airiness; others feel somewhat insecure in them. If you go the wire route, choose the kind with heavy-gauge epoxy-coated wire.

A fold-up portable nylon mesh crate is perfect if you travel with your dog a lot. Most hotels require that your dog be crated while in the room—especially if you're not there as well. (The so-called "portable" wire crates aren't really very portable.) These nylon crates aren't great for diggers and chewers, but they are excellent for the well-behaved traveller. Choose the kind with water-resistant plastic for easier cleaning. The cost depends on the size.

Crate Comfort

The crate should be large enough for your dog to stand up and turn around in. You must therefore either buy a very large crate now (which can make housetraining more troublesome), or you'll need to "trade up" as your Weim grows. One possible solution is to buy a crate with removable barriers; that way, you can progressively enlarge the crate. And unless you don't mind dismantling and lugging a heavy crate all around the house, consider getting two.

To help your Weim view his crate in a positive light, make it cosy and inviting. Furnish it with comfortable bedding and toys. Allow your youngster free access in and out of the enclosure for as much of the day as possible. When he has to be confined, do it for only short periods of time and hang around so that he'll know he isn't alone. Never use the crate as a place of punishment. Praise him (or even give him a treat) whenever he seeks out the crate on his own.

For dogs who like crates, an enclosure can be comforting during thunderstorms or if they are forced into an unwelcome separation from their humans. Dogs who dislike crates, however, will suffer much more when forced into one. Some will even destroy the crate in a frantic effort to escape.

In any case, crating your Weim for more than three hours at a time is not healthy. He needs exercise and attention. Make the crate a den, not a prison.

Food and Water Bowls

Choose durable (not plastic) bowls made of stainless steel or ceramic. Plastic bowls can develop minute cracks that allow bacteria to grow and thrive; they also can irritate a dog's chin, causing dermatitis and chin acne. Stainless steel bowls are inexpensive and durable. Ceramic bowls are very handsome, but they can be costly and easily breakable.

You can purchase weighted bowls to make spills less likely.

Grooming Equipment

Buy the best quality equipment that you can afford; in fact, shop the catalogues and buy implements designed for groomers. You won't regret the investment. Have at the ready:

- brushes or grooming mitt
- combs
- dental supplies (toothbrush and made-for-dogs toothpaste)
- nail clippers, nail file, and styptic powder
- shampoo

Pick out safe, size-appropriate toys for your puppy.

ID

Each year, more than 10 million pets are lost. Don't let yours be one of them. It's absolutely critical to get ID for your Weimaraner as soon as possible, which is not the same as when you get around to it.

The best ID for your Weim comprises a traditional collar tag *plus* a tattoo or microchip. The collar provides the simplest and most visible protection, while the tattoo or microchip is permanent. Collar tags should include your name, address, and phone number. Collars can get lost, so you need a second line of defence like the microchip or tattoo.

Tattoos

A tattoo can be registered with a company which will contact you if your dog is found.

You also can have a contact number tattooed right on the dog, but you had better be sure that the information won't change.

Microchip

A microchip is very small, about the size of a grain of rice. It is inserted with a needle in the back of the pet's neck. When a scanner is passed over it, it reads out a number that is registered with the microchip company. The company keeps the owner's contact information.

The only drawback to this method of identification is if the person doing the scanning is not careful, she could miss the microchip. The pet needs to be thoroughly scanned to pick up the chip.

Lead

In addition to a collar, the other essential neckwear item for your dog is a nylon or leather lead. A 6-foot (1.8 m) lead should be all that you need to walk your Weim safely. Many shops offer matching leads and collars. Just make sure that the lead feels comfortable in your hand.

Toys

Your chew-oriented Weimaraner will enjoy a variety of chew toys. Select some that are suitable for his size and remove any hanging strings, buttons, or other items that could pose a danger. Stuffed toys, squeaky toys, rope toys, and rawhides are best given

Dog Dens

Although you might not like to be confined to a small room, both wild and domestic canines often seek the security of small dens where nothing can sneak up on them. In fact, most dogs enjoy the den-like environment of their crates because it makes them feel safe.

Retractable Leads

While I find them a bit heavy and awkward to use, some people like retractable leads. But if you like the idea of allowing your dog more freedom, by all means indulge yourself. However, remember that they are not meant for high-traffic zones!

only under supervision. Dogs belong to one of two chewing schools: chewers and gulpers. If your Weim is a chewer, he is probably going to be all right handling rawhides, because he will patiently chew them into manageable fragments. Gulpers, on the other hand, simply swallow down large amounts at once, risking a blockage. And while bones and rawhide pose problems for nearly all dogs, gulpers are at extra risk.

Any Weimaraner worth his salt can remove the squeaker from a toy in about six seconds, so it's essential to supervise your Weim if you decide to give him a squeaker toy. Avoid cow hooves because they can be harder than your dog's tooth enamel and are frequently responsible for tooth breakage. They also can splinter and cause choking. I would also avoid toys with batteries, because your Weim may be able to remove the batteries from the toy, and swallow or chew on them.

Weims love balls, but their powerful teeth and jaws can make mincemeat of all but the toughest balls in a matter of seconds. Your dog could then choke on the pieces. Play it safe and invest in a tough polyurethane ball from a pet shop. The "balls on a rope" are also fantastic. The rope allows you throw the ball much farther—and you won't get dog slobber all over your hands.

Dogs who need long-term activity

Make sure you provide your Weim with appropriate chew toys.

enjoy toys that can be stuffed with cheese or peanut butter—the challenge is to extract the food!

A MEMBER OF THE FAMILY

When you get your Weim, prepare to welcome him into your family. Gone are the days when the family dog was banished to a life in the back garden. The American Animal Hospital Association (AAHA) conducted a survey of 1,238 United States and Canadian pet owners' attitudes toward their pets, and here's what they found:

- Sixty-nine percent break household rules with their pet (such as letting the pet up on the bed) when their spouse or significant other is not present.
- If they were left on a desert island and could choose only one companion, 50 percent said they would pick a pet rather than a human being.
- Fifty-three percent are spending more on their pets now than they did three years ago.
- Ninety-three percent say they would risk their own life for their pet.
- Ninety-four percent take their pet for regular veterinary checkups to ensure their pet's quality of life.
- Fifty-eight percent reported their pet got more frequent medical care than they did.

Obviously, the addition of such an important member of the family requires special planning. Preparation is critical for any pet, but Weimaraners require more preparation than most. Poor planning on your part leads to problem behaviours on the part of the dog—and the ugly fact is that more dogs are euthanised for problem behaviours than for any other reason.

Many people underestimate just how much care, especially exercise, a Weimaraner needs. Too many people think that the cure for an excited dog is to stick him in a crate—not run him for an hour.

Introducing a New Dog

It's tempting to get a new puppy as a "companion" to an older dog, especially with the thought that when the older one passes away, you'll still have a young dog to comfort you. And while this scenario may work out, be cautious. Many older dogs

Raw Reality

Rawhides have no nutritional value whatsoever. They are also full of artificial preservatives and colouring.

45

are settled in their ways, and if they lead a sedentary lifestyle, a young, bouncing puppy (a Weimaraner of all things!) may make your older dog's golden years turn to rust pretty fast. This is the kind of situation when you might consider getting an adult dog from a rescue group—you'll still have a companion for you and your dog but one who will be less likely to produce grey hairs in both of you. And if you have the choice, pick a dog of the opposite sex from the one you now have.

Even in the best of circumstances, a difficult transition period may ensue. Unless there is serious fighting with blood drawn, the dogs will settle affairs between themselves. It may be best to introduce the two dogs on neutral ground, off lead if possible. This gives them the best chance to meet, sniff, and play before being brought together in the resident dog's permanent home, where he is more likely to display territoriality toward any stranger. The new dog will still probably be considered a suspect—but perhaps a bit less so. Observe their behaviour carefully. Wagging tails don't necessarily mean hail-fellow-well-met; it can be a prelude to a fight.

In most cases, dogs will sort things out pretty amicably. (See Chapter 6 for ways to keep the peace if they don't get along well.)

With proper introductions, your Weim can get along with other dogs.

Dog Meets Cat

Weimaraners have a strong prey drive that doesn't often endear them to cats. However, if you already have a strong, sensible cat, you may be able to bring home a Weim puppy who will grow up in a household ruled by the feline species. However, make sure that the cat always has a place to escape to, and supervise the pair carefully.

We all know that cats and dogs are not natural buddies. They are both top-level predators, competing for territory, affection, and food. In a straightforward battle, a determined dog will win, but the cunning cat makes up for his relative weakness and small size with a depth of slyness and bravado lacking in the average mutt. The Weimaraner, however, is not the average mutt. Equally cunning, strong, fast, and possessed of a powerful prey drive, a Weim can easily overpower his smaller rival.

Your Weim and your cat will probably never be best friends, but it may be possible to lull them into a state of mutual avoidance. If your Weim has been raised with cats from puppyhood, your chances of making him open to a friendship with your own cats are vastly improved. If he has not been raised with cats, you may still win them over, but be aware that you may in the end be forced to give up one or the other for the safety of the cat. It is more likely that the dog will show altogether too much interest in the cat, in which case you may have to simply keep them on separate floors.

During the introduction period, make sure that the cat is safe and that the dog is under control. Keep them apart at first so that they can see but not touch each other, and gradually allow them closer proximity for longer periods of time. If the day ever comes when they actually sleep together, you are probably home free.

Toy Tip

Don't put out all your Weimaraner's toys at once; rotate them so that your highly intelligent dog doesn't get bored.

Dogs and Babies

Your Weim and your baby can become excellent friends with the right introductions. It is important to remember at all times that many Weims have a high prey drive, and until your dog knows better, he may regard a new baby as a succulent feast or catchable quarry, not as a member of his family. For this reason, *never* leave your dog alone with a small child. Just play it safe. The situation is even more fraught with peril if you do not have a firm grasp on leadership.

How Much Can You Handle?

Some people would enjoy adding a second or even third Weimaraner to the household. Your ability to do this depends partly on the temperament of the first dog but also on your own availability, energy, and resources. If your one dog is not getting enough companionship now, adding a second will only divide your time further. That said, some people do manage to have multiple dogs!

GOING PLACES

More owners are travelling with their Weims than ever before, and the travel industry is taking notice. Pet-friendly hotels, parks, and campgrounds are gaining ground. There are even travel agents who specialise in putting vacations together for owners and their adventurous pooches.

If you do travel with your Weim, keep his safety in mind at all times And always, always be respectful of others—this includes cleaning up after your dog and making sure that he is well mannered and well behaved in new and often overwhelming situations.

By Car

You must secure your Weim when in the car. Get him accustomed to riding in his crate or fastened in with a doggy seatbelt. A dog bouncing around the car is certain to get hurt in the event of an accident or even if you need to stop short. Also, you don't need to have your dog jumping in your lap while you're driving.

Most dogs seem to like to ride in the car, but there's an exception to every rule. If your Weim gets carsick, there could be two reasons: physical nausea or fear. (And the causes can exacerbate each other.)

Some Weims have high prey drives, and wouldn't be suitable for a house with small animals.

Packing for Poochie

Wherever you go, you'll need to pack (more than you think) for your dog. The well-travelled Weimaraner is accompanied by:

- dog seatbelt or crate
- ID tags
- food and water bowls
- gingersnap biscuits to alleviate carsickness
- extra water
- food supply and tin opener (if applicable)
- brush, toothbrush, and toothpaste
- bedding
- toys and treats

- first-aid kit
- health certificate and vet records
- list of 24-hour animal clinics in the area you'll be going to
- photos of your Weim — one for your wallet and one in your suitcase
- medications
- poop bags and paper towels
- cleaner

If your dog seems afraid, try just petting and playing with him in the car (without actually going anywhere), then let him out. Don't sympathise with his fear—you want him to understand what a fun thing you're doing! Then, take several short trips to a pleasant place like a park and walk around. Slow down around corners; you reduce his chances of vomiting if you do, and you may save your own neck as well. Opening a window may help, as may turning on the air conditioning.

By Air

Airlines are continually updating their regulations for carrying pets, so the first thing you'll need to do when contemplating air travel is to check with the airline. Here, however, are a few tips to make a trip easier on you and your Weimaraner:

- Go with a known airline or reputable pet transport company. Don't trust your precious Weim to some fly-by-night outfit.
- Don't feed your Weim within six hours of departure or give him
water within two hours of departure.
- If possible, book a nonstop flight to reduce stress. Don't book any flight that requires a change of planes.
- Most airlines require a health certificate no more than ten days old before the flight. You can get one from your vet.
- If you can't get your Weim in the cabin with you (and you

An exercise pen can come in handy when you are travelling with your Weim.

probably can't), be sure that he goes as luggage, not freight. This will increase the chances that he gets off when you do. Book travel for morning or evening flights to avoid extreme temperatures that may occur in the heat of day or cold of night.

• Confirm your reservations the day before the flight.

• Don't medicate your dog with tranquilizers before the flight. They can repress his breathing mechanisms and promote heat loss.

• Use an airport-approved crate, and make sure that it is clearly identified.

• Tip the baggage handlers—well.

• Notify the gate personnel that your dog needs to be unloaded as soon as possible—ahead of inanimate luggage.

WHEN YOUR WEIM CAN'T COME WITH YOU

You can't always take your dog everywhere you go. Sometimes a trusted friend or neighbour can take on the pet-sitting responsibility, but other times you'll have to go the professional route.

Pet Sitters

If you decide to hire a pet sitter, look for one who's licensed and insured, and get references. You also can ask your vet for references. Whomever you pick should be able to provide you with a brochure that lists services and states fees. You should have the pet sitter visit your home before you leave so that you can give her details about any special care that your dog may need. It's not a good sign if the pet sitter is late for this meeting.

During the first meeting, observe the pet sitter's interaction with your dog. She should show friendliness and confidence. She should understand the Weimaraner's special nature and be well informed about potential health emergencies such as bloat. Be sure to leave information about how (and when) to contact your vet.

For further information to help you find the right petsitter for you see the resources section of this book.

Boarding Kennels

In some cases, the best solution for care when you're away is a boarding kennel.

Before you make a reservation, visit the kennel to make sure that it suits your needs. You may want to start with a telephone interview. Ask how long the facility has been in business, and request references. Then call them. Of course you will ask about fees, but the cheapest is not always the best. (Neither is the most expensive, though.)

Inquire about whether you can bring your dog's toys and bedding. Familiar items and odours will make him feel more at home. Some kennels will allow you to leave your dog's lead there; others will ask you to take it home with you.

Your dog will be required to be up to date on vaccinations, but which ones depend on the kennel. Find out what the facility requires and arrive prepared with records of the vaccinations in hand. To ensure your Weimaraner will be safe (and to satisfy the requirements of most kennels) keep his immunisations current. For the greatest efficacy, vaccinations should be given at least a week before boarding—the body doesn't develop immunity immediately.

Make a surprise visit to the kennel. It should look and smell clean. The staff should be friendly, kind, and knowledgeable. Ask them what experience they have had with Weims, and ask if they are familiar with the signs of bloat. Also ask about the feeding and exercise schedule. Inquire about how your Weimaraner's considerable exercise needs will be met. Some kennels have playtime in which several well-mannered dogs can enjoy each others' company. If your kennel has this practice, make sure that it is supervised. If you are worried about inter-dog aggression, you may want to opt out of this activity (dog-to-dog hostilities can arise at even the best run kennel). Ask about food; you may want to bring your own, especially because some dogs experience vomiting and diarrhoea when their diet is changed.

Reserve your Weim's place in the kennel as far ahead as possible, especially if you will be gone over the holidays. Get a copy of his medical records and give a copy to the kennel. Also

Easing the Stress of Travel

Many people have had success with diphenhydramine (Benadryl), an over-the-counter antihistamine, to relax their dogs and make them tired before a flight. Give your dog a dose at home first to see how he responds. (Dosage depends on your dog's weight. Consult your veterinarian before giving any medication to your dog.)

leave his tags and microchip numbers. If your Weim has special needs or requires medication, give written instructions to the kennel staff that include the dosage and frequency. The kennel should have your contact information and that of your vet as well. You may want to leave them your credit card number in case of a vet emergency (or let them know that the vet has the number).

If you must leave your Weim behind, a pet sitter may be a good choice.

Pet-Friendly Hotels

Don't take chances. Believe it or not, not every hotel in the world will welcome your Weimaraner. They have not yet received the word that he's the best dog on earth. So call ahead to verify that the hotel currently accepts pets. Just because they did last year doesn't mean that they do this year. I stayed in a dog-friendly hotel a few years ago—at least it *was* dog friendly—until one of the other guests decided to allow her dog to swim in the hotel pool. The establishment is no longer dog friendly, and it wasn't even the dog's fault.

Even hotels that welcome pets may have limits on the size of dog allowed or the number of dogs permitted. Some require that the dog remain crated if left alone in the room. Some require an extra deposit or charge additional cleaning fees.

Make sure that you and your Weim never leave the hotel room unless he is on a lead. Even if he is perfectly trained to stay by your side, leads are the rule. Other guests may be afraid of dogs, and the lead is reassuring to them. And of course, clean up after your dog after every outing. Don't allow him to bark or scratch at the door. If you have to, keep him safely in a crate.

Chapter

4

FEEDING

Your Weimaraner

Nutrition is a cornerstone of good health. It affects the way your dog looks, feels, and behaves. A dog on a healthy diet has a great-looking coat, a clean scent, lots of energy, and a strong immune system.

When dogs were wolves, they managed to find proper (although sometimes inadequate) nutrition on their own. Nowadays they depend totally upon you. Your nutritional choices for your dog determine to a large extent how healthy and happy he will be. This is not a responsibility to take lightly.

In 1985, the National Research Council (NRC) established the basic nutrient needs of dogs, but it left wide (and sometimes critical) margins. The NRC nutritional requirements are *not* based on optimum levels. They are intended to cover the "average" needs of healthy dogs. Between 5 and 10 percent of all dogs require more or less than the NRC-calculated average. There is a big difference between the *minimum* a dog needs to survive (the minimum daily requirement, or MDR) and the *recommended* daily allowance (RDA). (There is also a *maximum* level—the amount over which a substance may be toxic.) Most good commercial foods provide the RDA.

Browse the shelves of any pet shop or supermarket, and you'll find commercial foods for dogs from every walk of life. Do a little research, and you'll find hundreds of books, websites, and the Internet discussion lists that discuss raw and homemade diets. You can be sure that no matter what you give your dog to eat, someone will be happy to tell you what's wrong with what you're feeding him.

With all of these types of diets and varying opinions, how can you ensure that your Weimaraner's diet is healthy? You don't need a degree in nutrition, but you do need to choose intelligently and be aware that your dog really is, in part at least, what he eats. Learn the fundamentals of canine nutrition and how to evaluate your dog's condition as it relates to his diet. Be aware, too, that if your dog develops a problem–lack of energy, dry skin and coat, itchiness, or chronic diarrhoea, for instance–it may be food related.

You dog's food needs may vary from day to day.

LET'S TALK NUTRIENTS

A nutrient is a dietary component that has a particular function. Nutrients that the body can manufacture on its own from other nutrients are called "nonessential." Those that the body needs to import in their final form are called "essential."

Nutrients perform one or more of the following functions:

- provide energy
- act as structural components
- take part in the chemical activities of the body
- transport substances around the body
- maintain body temperature

There are six basic classes of nutrients and about 45 specific substances that your dog needs to survive. The former are carbohydrates, fats, minerals, proteins, vitamins, and water. Of these, proteins, fats, and carbohydrates provide energy. Water, minerals, and vitamins, although necessary for survival, do not supply energy.

The nutrients that your dog needs work synergistically. For example, a specific metabolic reaction may take ten steps, each requiring a different nutrient. If even one of these nutrients is missing or deficient, it's as though all ten are missing.

Carbohydrates

Sugars and starches are both carbohydrates, a nutrient that comes primarily from plants. In fact, in the raw state, between 60 and 90 percent (excluding water) of a plant is made up of carbohydrates.

There is no minimum dietary level of carbohydrates in the canine diet. However, when present, they perform the following functions (that also can be performed by proteins and fats):

- provide energy
- supply a heat source for the body
- serve as building blocks for other biological components,

such as glycoproteins, vitamin C, nonessential amino acids, glycolipids, and lactose

- can be stored as glycogen or converted to fat
- help to regulate protein and fat metabolism

Fats

Fats have twice the number of calories per gram as proteins or carbohydrates; they are packed with energy. They keep cells in good working order and add both palatability and texture to food. Dogs digest fats *very* efficiently, better than they digest carbohydrates or protein.

The proper diet will keep your Weim looking and feeling good.

Dogs can use both plant and animal fats with equal ease. However, oils derived from plants provide large amounts of essential fatty acids (EFAs), which are required for many biological functions.

Performance dogs need more fat in their diets than a sedentary Weimaraner. These dogs also need a highly digestible meat protein. Quality food is less wasteful, in more senses than one, because it produces less faeces. Less scooping equals more fun!

Minerals

A dietary mineral is any inorganic component of a food. Like vitamins, minerals are substances necessary for an animal's health. Minerals participate in nearly every function of the body. They build teeth and bone, serve as parts of enzymes, and are a vital part of the blood and other body fluids. Minerals also play a role in muscle contraction, the transmission of nerve impulses, and in cell membrane permeability.

Dietary minerals are generally classed into two main groups: macrominerals (sulphur, calcium, phosphorus, magnesium, and the electrolytes sodium, potassium, and chloride), which are consumed in gram quantities per day, and trace minerals (including iron, zinc, copper, iodine, and selenium), which are needed in milligrams or micrograms per day. A third class includes the ultratrace minerals, which have been shown to be necessary in laboratory animals but not specifically in dogs. As with vitamins, do not add mineral

An Enhanced Diet for Performance

A performance diet should have a highly digestible, quality protein source, such as a specific kind of meat as its first ingredient. To help a dog get off to a good start nutritionally, owners should begin feeding a performance diet several weeks — ideally from 8 to 12 weeks — before training begins.

supplements to your dog's diet without consulting your veterinarian.

Proteins

Proteins are long, complex molecules of amino acids that are strung together like beads on a chain. They compose about 50 percent of every cell. Proteins are critical in building enzymes, hormones, haemoglobin, and antibodies. All animals need protein for maintenance, and young animals need it for growth. If a puppy doesn't get enough protein, his tissues and organs won't develop properly. Dogs also use protein for energy. Dogs with cancer, trauma, and burns need additional protein to help them heal.

Vitamins

According to *Stedman's Medical Dictionary*, a vitamin is "one of a group of organic substances, present in minute amounts in natural foodstuffs, that are essential to normal metabolism." Vitamins are naturally present only in tiny amounts, but they are critical for life.

Both dogs and people need vitamins for thousands of chemical reactions that take place in the body. Along with minerals, vitamins help digestion, reproduction, blood clotting, and the normal development of muscle, bone, skin, and hair. Vitamins serve as parts of enzymes and are important in helping the body use protein, carbohydrates, and fats.

Vitamins come in two major varieties: fat soluble and water soluble. Fat-soluble vitamins can be stored by the body, but water-

Supplementing Your Dog's Diet

The supplement industry is big—there's no doubt about it. In the past few years the market has grown 3,000 percent. And while it is usually true that if a healthy dog is getting good food, supplements are not needed, the problem is that even canine nutritionists are not completely sure what makes a food "good." In addition, not all dogs are completely healthy—in which case it may make sense to add a little something extra to the diet.

Do *not* supplement minerals like calcium or phosphorus except at the direction of your veterinarian. Supplementing the already carefully balanced minerals in your dog's food can lead to trouble. The same is true of certain fat-soluble vitamins like A and D; these vitamins are stored in the liver and can be toxic in large doses. (Vitamin E, another fat-soluble vitamin, does not appear to have toxic effects and may be supplemented if desired.)

However you may feel about supplements, they are not all equal—even when you consider the same supplement. Before you buy, check out the source. Use a product that was designed for animals, even if it uses human-grade ingredients, as it should. You also should look for organically grown herbs where possible.

soluble vitamins are excreted quickly and should be supplied every day in the diet.

Water

Water is the most important substance of all. It carries nutrients, flushes waste, aids certain chemical reactions, helps to regulate body temperature, and provides shape and resilience to the body.

About 70 percent of your dog's lean body mass *is* water. (With drooling breeds, it's even higher.) The percentage of water present in your dog's body depends somewhat on how fat he is. Lean dogs have a *higher* percentage of water than fat ones, because fat contains less water than muscle tissue. Lean dogs also need proportionately more water than heavy dogs because they eat more food per unit of body weight.

Your dog maintains his water balance by water intake and metabolic water production (making water from his food). Water is lost through panting and toileting.

Always have a fresh supply of water out for your Weim.

The following factors can influence your dog's need for water:

- ambient temperature
- food type and amount
- exercise
- certain diseases
- lactation

Unless your vet advises you to, don't restrict your dog's access to water, even if you think he doesn't really need as much as he is drinking. (One exception may be when housetraining your puppy; you may limit his water access for an hour or so before bedtime.) Your Weimaraner needs constant access to clean, fresh water. If you have more than one Weimaraner, give each dog a separate dish.

COMMERCIAL FOODS

We have only been feeding our dogs processed feeds, at least on a large scale, for about 60 years. (The military played a role in the popularisation of manufactured dog food because the army needed a convenient, easy-to-store food for its dogs of war.) Nowadays, about 95 percent of dog owners feed their dogs primarily or solely a commercial diet, usually dry kibble. While most of these products contain the minimum amounts of nutrients to be considered "nutritionally complete," none of them are really ideal foods for your dog. Their greatest advantage is that they are convenient, and they do give your dog adequate nutrition. In fact, a dog on a commercial diet probably eats as well as you do. Take that for what it's worth.

Types of Commercial Food

Dry Food (Kibble)

Kibble is a convenient, nutritionally adequate food for dogs. Dry food helps to reduce tartar buildup on teeth but not as much as actually brushing the teeth does. And it doesn't do anything for cleaning the canine teeth (the fangs) because chewing (if any) is done with the back teeth.

In comparison with other food choices, dry food is the least expensive, largely because of its high grain content. Dry food tends to be low in fat, which is good if your dog is overweight or inactive. Don't be seduced by fancy colours and shapes, though. Shape doesn't matter, and the colours come from vegetable dye, not food nutrients.

Most, but not all, dry foods are preserved with BHA or BHT. Although BHA and BHT have been established as safe, many people question this finding. If you don't wish to feed your dog food containing these preservatives, you can find some dry foods

Keeping Your Weim Young and Spry

The National Institute on Ageing (NIA) funded a study that tested the benefits of exercise and a diet fortified with antioxidant vitamins, fruits, and vegetables. The study divided 48 older dogs (between the ages of 8 and 11) into four groups. One group got a twice-weekly workout, a regular rotation of toys, lived in a kennel with a roommate, and "went to school" to learn how to find hidden treats. Another group ate a diet rich in antioxidants but enjoyed none of the lifestyle benefits of the first group. A third group got both the antioxidant diet and the lifestyle benefits. And the last group got no special treatment. The supplements included tomatoes, carrot granules, citrus pulp, and spinach flakes.

It revealed (not shockingly) that an antioxidant diet actually helped older dogs learn new tricks and kept them spry. They discovered that dogs who were given either the fortified diet, regular exercise, or both did much better in learning new tricks than dogs who were fed regular chow and who were allowed to lie around.

In short, exercise and a diet that includes fruits and vegetables get better results than just feeding a dog kibble out of a bag and letting him lie around all day.

that don't use them. However, they are pricey and sometimes hard to locate.

Commercial kibble comes in several sizes. Some research has shown that larger size kibble is less likely to be a factor in bloat, a dangerous emergency condition of the digestive system.

Some people like to feed their dogs a basic diet of kibble, with different added foods every day, like green beans, carrots, gravy, or tinned meat. This plan gives your dog adequate nutrition and variety.

Soy

Soy is a protein that many dogs are allergic to; stay away from it.

Tinned Food

Although some tinned dog food smells unpleasant to humans (one reason that most people prefer to serve kibble), most dogs prefer both the aroma and flavour of tinned foods. In fact, some people serve such unappetising dry fare that they have to anoint the stuff with tinned food before their dogs will touch it. To find the best tinned food for your dog, look for food containing whole meat, fish, or poultry as the first ingredient. Most lower quality tinned foods have water as the first ingredient.

Unfortunately, the top tinned foods often cannot be found at your supermarket. Instead, you must go to the manufacturer, a few pet specialty shops, or dog shows. This is because the high shelf rental space of most supermarkets is out of the reach of many small premium pet food manufacturers.

Tinned food is much more expensive than kibble, and it is usually about 75 percent water. Tinned foods are also high in fat. They can be useful for mixing with dry food, however, because most dogs find them highly palatable. Dogs who have urinary tract infections often thrive better on tinned dog foods than on kibble, mostly because of the increased water in tinned foods.

If you're feeding a commercial diet, look for a high-quality food.

Some tinned dog foods contain grain products, while others have only meat. Whether or not grain products are good for dogs is controversial. The best tinned foods use whole vegetables, not grain fractions like rice bran, rice flour, and brewer's rice. Dogs need a vegetable element in their diet, so if you feed a pure meat dinner, supplement it with dog biscuits or fresh vegetables.

Semi-Moist Food

Semi-moist food is about 25 percent water and can be just as high in sugar in the form of corn syrup, beet pulp, sucrose, and caramel. Your dog does not need this stuff, which promotes obesity and tooth decay. The shelf life of these products is also lower than either tinned or dry food.

Reading the Label

Most owners prefer the convenience of buying ready-prepared dog foods, rather than preparing homecooked balanced meals, so it is important to understand exactly what you are buying.

All commercial dog foods should meet a minimum nutritional requirement. In the UK, pet food is controlled by the Food Standards Agency (FSA), which has to adhere to EC guidelines. Pet food manufacturers also belong to the Pet Food Manufacturers Association (PFMA), which, in turn, follows guidelines laid down by the European Pet Food Industry Federation.

One of the biggest favours you can do for your Weimaraner

What's In a Name?

There are all kinds of arcane rules about how companies can name their foods. Most consumers don't know the rules, so it doesn't do them much good, but the rules are something like this: To call something "Diane's Ostrich Dog Food," at least 95 percent of the product must be ostrich (not counting water). If you count water, then at least 70 percent of the product must be the meat listed. If I decide to combine two meats, together, they must add up to 95 percent, with the ingredient listed first predominant. So if I sell "Diane Octopus and Giraffe Dog Food," there has to be more octopus than giraffe, and it all has to total 95 percent.

But let's say I don't have that much meat to put in the food I am selling. If I have more than 25 percent but less than 95 percent, then I can't called it "Ostrich Dog Food" any more—but I can call it "Diane's Ostrich Dinner," or "Diane's Ostrich Entrée," or "Diane's Ostrich Nuggets." And it could mean that I threw in some octopus too. Or emu.

So maybe I don't have even that much ostrich meat. Maybe I have only between 3 and 25 percent. Then I have to say something like "Diane's Special Dog Food Dinner With Ostrich." Get it? "Diane's Ostrich Dog Food" is 95 percent ostrich. "Diane's Dog Food With Ostrich" might be only 3 percent ostrich. If I don't even have that much, I can say that it's flavoured with ostrich.

is to read the label of ingredients on dog food before buying it. But reading it isn't enough; you need to understand what each ingredient is, what the source of the ingredient might be, and what the possible long-term health consequences could be of consuming some substances on a regular basis.

The information that is detailed on a food label follows guidelines given by the Foods Standards Agency, working with the Pet Food Manufacturer's Association. Every label must contain the following information:

- Typical Analysis. The percentage of the following must be listed: proteins, oils and fats, fibre, moisture (when it exceeds 14 percent), ash (this represents the mineral content of the food and is determined by the burning of the product).
- Ingredients List. The ingredients must be listed in descending order by weight. They can be indicated using category names laid down by the Regulations (e.g. 'meat and animal derivatives', 'derivatives of vegetable origin'). Alternatively, ingredients can be listed by individual names. When an ingredient is used that does not fall into any of the prescribed categories, its individual name must be listed. In all other circumstances, mixing individual names and category names is not permitted. If particular attention is drawn to a specific ingredient (e.g. "With Chicken"), the percentage of that ingredient component must also be listed.
- Additives. If preservatives, antioxidants or colourants have been added to the product their presence has to be declared using category or chemical names, in accordance with the Feeding Stuffs Regulations.
- Vitamins. If Vitamins A, D and E are added to the product, their presence and level has to be declared. The level must include both the quantity naturally present in the raw materials and the quantity added. The Regulations also lay down the units that must be used to declare the level.
- Best Before Date. This date indicates the minimum storage life of the product. The month and year must be shown.
- Bar Code. This is not a legal requirement but allows for information about sales, stocks, etc.
- Batch Number. A batch number or the date of manufacture must be given to facilitate traceability of the product. This may be given either in the statutory statement or it might be printed

Grazing in the Grass

Alas, no one really knows why dogs eat grass. They can't digest the stuff, after all. They may just like the taste, or they may perceive it as some kind of needed fibre in their diet. Some dogs may eat it to clear their stomach because it will make them vomit.

Unfortunately, just because a product has "beef" as the first ingredient doesn't mean that the product is mostly beef. Most companies engage in a practice known as "splitting." If they can possibly do so, they will divide the cereal products into separate categories like "rice," "rice bran," and then "brown rice." Added together, there may be more rice than beef. But because the companies are allowed to list them separately, beef is listed first.

elsewhere on the package/label/container, in which case the statutory statement shall indicate where it can be found.

- Net Weight. The net weight must be given in accordance with the Feeding Stuffs Regulations 2002. The Weights and Measures (Packaged Goods) Regulations 1986 lays down the exact marking and size of lettering required.
- Name and Address. This is the name and address of the company responsible for the products. It may be a manufacturer, packer, importer, seller or distributor.

ALTERNATIVES TO COMMERCIAL FOOD

Before dog food came in tins and pouches, we fed our dogs *something*. If you have the time and the inclination, you might want to prepare your Weim's diet yourself.

Is Human Food Okay?

If you listened to the pet food companies, you'd be convinced that serving your dog a mouthful of turkey breast would set him on an unrecoverable journey to malnutrition and disease. The truth is that you can feed your dog healthy "people food" like turkey, chicken, and beef, along with (if you desire) good carbohydrates. Dogs don't actually need carbs in their diet—they are the original Atkins animals—but they can use them. The only caveat, especially with young dogs, is that you must be careful to supply calcium and phosphorus in the proper ratio. Not doing so can lead to poor bone development and disease. The easiest way around this dilemma is to feed your puppy a good commercial food. (Go ahead and mix 'em up—variety is good for dogs.) When your puppy gets older, you can switch to homemade if you want. For complete information, see my book *Feeding Your Dog for Life.*

Homemade Diet

Cooking for dogs is not rocket science. While it can be a bit challenging to cook for a puppy, with an adult dog it's fairly easy to prepare dinner at home. A normal healthy dog's diet should consist of one-third cooked meat or eggs, one-third cooked carbohydrates like rice, grains, or pasta, and one-third cooked green and yellow vegetables like carrots or broccoli (but not onions). For added nutrition, you can add some brewer's yeast (debittered), wheat

germ, or powdered kelp. Voilá.

Plenty of books are available if you are interested in feeding your dog a homemade diet. Of course, talk to your vet before you start your Weim on any new diet.

Raw Diet

Raw diets, sometimes referred to as BARF (Bones and Raw Food), include uncooked meaty bones, uncooked muscle and organ meat, raw eggs, vegetables, fruit, yogurt, cooked cereals, cottage cheese, and herbs, enzymes, and other supplements. Preparing a diet like this at home does require some training. If not prepared in the proper balance, dogs can have nutrient deficiencies. People who decide to feed their dogs a diet of fresh meat and vegetables without the bone must artificially supplement the food with a calcium source.

A great deal has been written lately about the advantages of a raw diet. However, it is best to check with your vet before making any major decisions that may affect your dog's diet.

There are some disadvantages to feeding your dog raw food, even if the meat supply is completely safe (and I don't believe that it is). Raw meat harbours organisms that can kill a dog. Common bacterial components of raw meat include campylobacterosis, *E. coli*, listeriosis, salmonellosis, trichinosis, and tapeworm. Protozoal infections are also possible. Cooking destroys those organisms. While it is true that cooking also destroys some important enzymes as well, dogs actually can make these enzymes themselves, just as humans can.

Don't let anyone talk you into a "natural diet" for your Weim without first consulting your veterinarian.

VARYING THE DIET

Don't get trapped into feeding your dog only one food, even a good

Treats

The best treats are low in fat, tasty, and high in nutritional value. You can't do better than yummy vegetables like sweet baby carrots, broccoli, banana slices, and an apple wedge. Baking a bit of beef liver is good, too, if you can take the smell. I can't, but for some reason it doesn't bother Weimaraners a bit.

With a non-commercial diet, you can control what goes into your Weim's food.

Feeding and Bloat Prevention

Because Weimaraners are prone to bloat (a very serious condition described in greater detail in Chapter 8), it's better to feed three times a day if you possibly can. Frequent smaller meals have been shown to reduce the frequency of this life-threatening condition.

one. Here's why:

- It's unnatural. Dogs are hunters and scavengers by nature and are designed to feed upon a wide variety of foodstuffs.
- It's boring. Dogs don't like the same food day in and day out any more than we would.
- It may be unhealthy. Studies have not been done long enough on a large enough number of dogs to guarantee that any single food is completely adequate by itself.
- Feeding the same food all the time may cause allergies. Researchers believe that one of the best ways for your dog to avoid a food allergy is to consume a wide variety of foods from puppyhood on.
- It may be impossible to always feed your Weim the same food. What if your dog becomes allergic to something in the food, or the company goes out of business, or it changes the formula, or you are holidaying in Upper Horse Pasture Gully where Fifi's Special Braised Cuts of Hippopotamus With Sauce isn't available?

Vegetarian Dogs?

Although dogs are classed anatomically as carnivores (based on tooth structure rather than eating habits), they are really omnivores who thrive on a wide variety of foods. However, dogs usually do best on a meat-based diet, although there are a few cases on record of dogs being allergic to all kinds of meat and who have been "forced" to adapt to a vegetarian lifestyle. If you wish to do so, it is possible to feed your dog a vegetarian diet, especially if you include eggs and dairy. Otherwise, it's difficult to get the high-quality protein that dogs need. That said, some companies do manufacture balanced vegetarian diets for dogs.

The Raw Food Craze

The raw food crowd will have you believing that commercial food is poison and the only way to nurse your dog back to health is to start him on a regimen of raw chicken wings and alfalfa sprouts. Raw food is a "natural food" that delivers high-quality ingredients. It also delivers pathogens and other bacteria.

Let's get real. Commercial food is not poison. Quality commercial food (and there are some very good ones and some pretty bad ones) provide a good-quality diet for your dog. Not the best, but it's pretty good. Serving a quality commercial food will give dogs about the same kind of nutrition that most people get: not great and too fattening, but okay.

HOW OFTEN? HOW MUCH?

Puppies need to be fed more often than adults.

As I mentioned earlier, I find that commercial dog food labels tend to recommend overfeeding your dog. Let some common sense come into play when feeding your Weim.

Puppies

Puppies should be fed three times a day. Growing Weimaraner puppies need approximately twice as much volume of food per pound (kg) of their own body weight as do adults. Feed your Weim a food formulated for puppies until he is about nine months old. Then start feeding ¼ adult food and ¾ puppy food for a few days. At this point, change to ½ adult food and ½ puppy food. After a few more days, feed ¾ adult food and ¼ puppy food. After this, you can feed only adult food.

Adults

I recommend feeding most adult dogs twice a day. And while amount can vary considerably, 1 to 1.5 cups (check package for metric equivalent) of kibble per day is usually a good amount—adjust according to your dog's exercise habits and metabolism. Warning: It's very easy to overfeed this breed! The basic rule is that if you can see your dog's ribs, feed him more. If you can't feel them, feed him less.

VORACIOUS EATERS

The Weimaraner has been known to devour mobile phones, makeup, sausages still in the tin, then the tin, a leg from a barstool, and 14 birth control pills. This was just one dog but not an atypical one.

According to the British Veterinary Association (BVA) between 25 and 40 percent of all household pets are overweight. Like their owners, dogs have adopted a more sedentary lifestyle, and it's showing around the waistline. We just have a hard time resisting that pleading look! Like us, dogs are programmed to be hungry pretty much all the time. It's unfortunate by contemporary standards, but physiology just hasn't kept up with modern food production. Our ancestors, both canine and primate, worried about having too little to eat. Now we worry about having too much.

To prevent your dog from looking like he needs a gastric bypass, monitor his portions (you're the one who has access to the refrigerator), and make sure that he gets adequate exercise—which for a Weimaraner, is quite a lot. A healthy dog is a thin dog, although the reverse is not necessarily true, of course.

The Weimaraner should be lithe and muscular, and not just for aesthetic reasons. An overweight Weim is subject to diabetes,

"People" Food for People Only

Not everything that we ingest ourselves is good for dogs. (And a lot of it isn't good for humans, either). Avoid giving your dog the following foods:

Alcohol: a pleasant buzz for you can put your dog into a coma.

Baby food: may contain onion powder, which can cause anaemia in dogs.

Bones: can splinter and cause obstructions.

Cat food: not balanced for dogs.

Chocolate, coffee, and tea: contain theobromine and caffeine, which are toxic to dogs.

Citrus oil extracts: cause vomiting.

Eggs (raw): contain avidin that destroys biotin.

Fat trimmings: can cause pancreatitis.

Fish (raw): can result in a thiamine deficiency.

Garbage: can contain multiple toxins.

Grapes and raisins: can damage the kidneys.

Hops: can cause panting and seizures and even death.

Liver: large amounts cause vitamin A poisoning.

Macadamia nuts: can cause rear leg lameness.

Marijuana: depresses the nervous system.

Milk and dairy products: cause diarrhoea in some dogs.

Mushrooms: may contain toxins.

Onions and garlic: contain sulphides and disulphides that destroy red blood cells.

Peach and other fruit stones: cause intestinal obstruction.

Persimmons: seeds can cause intestinal blockage.

Salt (lots): causes electrolyte imbalances.

Sweets: cause obesity and dental problems.

Vitamins for people containing iron: can damage the stomach lining.

Yeast dough: can expand in the stomach.

A Weimaraner should be lithe and muscular.

orthopaedic problems, Cushing's disease, and cardiovascular disease. Don't allow your Weim to free-feed (which means leaving food out for him to consume as he desires). Some very well-done feeding trials have proven that dogs fed a free-choice diet versus an owner-restricted one have a higher incidence of orthopaedic problems—everything from hip dysplasia to anterior cruciate ligament ruptures. Other diseases are also more common.

Traditional weight-loss diet plans restrict fat intake, increase complex carbohydrates and fibre, and maintain the optimal amount of protein. Experimenters are trying out the more natural Atkins approach as well. Diets that have a severe restriction of calories (25 percent or greater) must be specially formulated and fortified to avoid nutritional imbalances. Special interest is being focused on L-carnitine, which appears to help dogs lose fat and maintain more muscle weight. Diets with L-carnitine are available by prescription.

Hormones and Weight Control

Some dogs are fat because of hormonal reasons. Check with your vet if you think that this is a possibility.

Chapter 5

GROOMING
Your Weimaraner

Grooming is much more than a home-beauty appointment. Done properly, it's a total health tune-up, a training process, and a great way for you to bond with your best friend. Although he requires a lot less work in this department than a Cocker Spaniel or a Poodle, your Weimaraner still has important grooming needs.

Grooming is also a time to check him out for bumps, growths, sores, and bruises. In addition, by removing dead and dirty hair and stimulating the skin, grooming helps your Weim avoid skin infections and irritations.

It is important to get your dog used to the idea of grooming. It is a strange feeling to a dog and can stress him out if he is the nervous type. Begin gradually if your dog seems unacquainted with the idea. Ideally, you should train your Weim to enjoy grooming early in his life, when he is a puppy, if possible.

BRUSHING

For regular brushing of the short-haired Weim, the only tool you really need is a natural bristle brush. If you're feeling lazy, a good brushing a twice a month will do the trick.

Brush with a bristle brush, and always brush the dog using the same pattern. (For example, if you start with the neck area and work down his body, make it a habit.) This gives your dog confidence because he knows what to expect next. Brush the coat down to the skin, but don't brush the skin itself. Doing so can cause brush burn—irritated, red skin that may require veterinary attention. Be gentle on tender areas, such as the belly and inside the legs. Rub the coat with a chamois to make the coat gleam. The long-haired variety needs to be combed before he's brushed and brushed before he's bathed.

A few people use scissors to trim away long hairs under the feet if necessary, but

A long-haired Weim will take a little bit longer to groom than the short-haired type.

it probably won't be for you. If you have a show dog, use "blending shears" to even out the coat where two different areas of hair growth meet in "seams." A professional groomer might even want to use a stripping knife to wring the last bit of gleam out of the coat; this is a tricky process that you should definitely leave to the pros.

BATHING

Bathing your Weim occasionally is good for him. It will not "destroy the oils" or "dry out" the oils in his coat—unless you're using lye.

Make sure that you have everything you need before bathing your dog. Nothing is worse than having a soaking wet dog in the bath and no shampoo at hand. Keep the following on hand:

- a warm, draft-free area
- bathing tether (if you're bathing your Weim in the bath)
- cotton balls
- hard rubber brush
- grooming mitt (optional)
- mineral oil
- rubber bath mat
- shampoo for dogs (formulated to the correct pH for his skin)
- sponge
- towels
- washcloth

Body Fat Check

A grooming session is a quick way to see if your Weim is too fat. Check his ribs, abdomen, and waist, areas where fat may accumulate. You should be able to feel your dog's ribs without pressing down really hard. If you can actually *see* his ribs, he is probably too thin.

Unless you have the rare long-haired variety, there are no mats and tangles to brush out first. It's right to the bath—and don't give your dog any clues about where you're heading. He'll figure it out soon enough on his own. In the unlikely event that your dog has gotten into tar or something equally horrid, trim out as much as you can and soak the area with mineral or vegetable oil for 24 hours before bathing.

Once you get your dog into the bath, put a drop of mineral oil in each eye to protect it from the shampoo, and pop a large cotton ball or some cotton batting in each ear.

Some people like to fill the bath to about the level of the dog's knees first. Use warm water, about 102°F (39°C), the dog's own temperature. Tether your Weim—have a clip to his collar attached to a suction cup to the wall, and then pour or spray the warm water over him slowly. When he's soaked, apply the shampoo to his back and lather gently for five or ten minutes. Avoid his face and mouth. To clean the face, use a washcloth or sponge. Be sure to clean his feet and nails as well. A brief session with a hard rubber brush during the bath will remove loose hair.

Next, drain the bath and rinse your dog thoroughly. Dry him with a towel or hair dryer on low. Keep him away from drafts until he is dry. At this point, you may want to use a grooming mitt to

Shedding

Considering that Weimaraners have hair less than 1 inch (2.5 cm) long, it's amazing how easily it falls out. This breed is an average but constant shedder. In addition, Weimaraners seem to produce more dandruff than you might expect, a fact that allergic people should note.

Everyone knows that lint rollers are excellent for picking up loose dog hair around the house. You also can use them directly on the dog. Lint rollers will get out the loose dirt, and what's more, dogs love them—apparently, they feel just like a massage.

Show dogs needs to be groomed and bathed to perfection.

73

remove dead hair. Once your Weim is bathed and dry, consider adding a light spray coat of conditioner or mink oil to give his coat a beautiful gloss.

EAR CARE

Your Weim's pendulous ears should be checked regularly. Swelling, discharge, redness, head shaking, pawing, or sensitivity to touch are all signs that there may be trouble brewing.

If your Weim's ears are dirty, use a commercial ear wash, preferably a natural one without alcohol. Massage the ear gently to get the wash into the whole ear. Massaging also helps to bring up all that waxy buildup, debris, and dirt. Don't use a cotton swab for this purpose—you might insert it too far and damage the ear. A cotton ball or soft cloth should be perfectly satisfactory. You may want to follow up with an ear powder to dry the ear and control odour.

Go Ahead —Mini-Poo!

It's fine to use a dry shampoo when you're in a hurry!

Check your Weim's ears regularly.

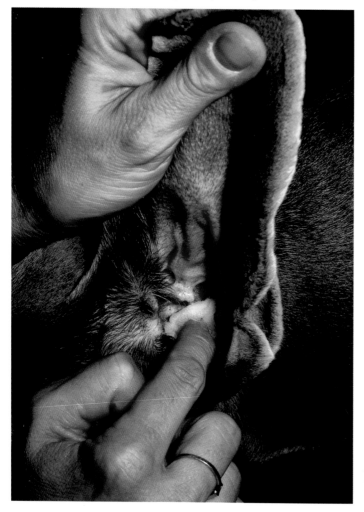

EYE CARE

Take a moment during the grooming process to examine your Weimaraner's eyes. After all, they are part of his charm! Cloudy or red eyes or eyes that are discharging mucus can mean trouble. Sunken, squinting, or protruding eyes are also suspicious. The pupils in both eyes should be the same size. And of course, if your dog has been pawing at his eyes, something is probably wrong. Any of these symptoms necessitate a call to the vet.

NAIL CARE

Trimming your dog's nails is an essential part of his good health. Long nails can easily catch in carpets or furniture and then break, resulting in bleeding. Long nails also can deform the foot, making walking difficult, and even grow into the paws, causing infections and abscesses. And if you don't trim the nails often enough, the vein in them can grow so long that you'll be able to get them back to the proper length only with great difficulty.

Still, the sad fact is that most dogs resent having their nails trimmed; it makes them nervous and insecure—especially if someone has previously cut a nail to the quick or pulled on a nail. The best thing is to start early and get your puppy used to you playing with and holding his feet.

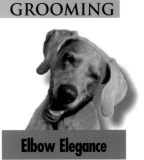

Elbow Elegance

Some Weims develop tough, calloused elbows. If this is the case with your dog, use an aloe skin cream moisturiser to soften them.

Anatomy of the Nail

The key to successful nail trimming is to understand the anatomy of the nail. Look carefully. Inside the centre of each nail is the "quick"—the blood and nerve supply. Fortunately, Weims are not supposed to have dark nails, which are much harder to trim because the quick isn't visible. It's very easy to see in clear white nails—it looks pinkish. In black nails, though, you have to make several tiny cuts to reduce the chances of nicking the quick. Trim away a bit at a time until you can just see a black dot in the centre of the nail as you look at it straight on. That's the tip of the quick. Trim no more today. One of the great things is that the more you trim, the more the quick will withdraw back into the nail and the less chance you'll have of nicking it.

Tools

Get your puppy used to nail trimming as soon as possible.

It's important to have the right instruments—in this case, a nail trimmer specifically designed for dogs. You can use either pliers-type or guillotine-type clippers, whichever you prefer. I like the pliers-type myself. In either case, make sure they're sharp! Many people also like to use an electric nail grinder, such as a Dremel tool. And oddly enough, once they get used to the noise, dogs seem to prefer them as well. Because they can heat up, be careful not to use electric nail grinders for too long a period.

If you're lucky, you'll have one of those super Weims who will sit quietly while you clip the nails. Others need to be restrained. In any case,

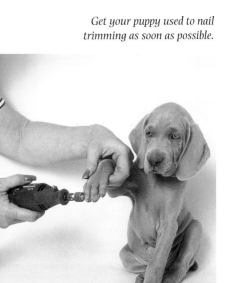

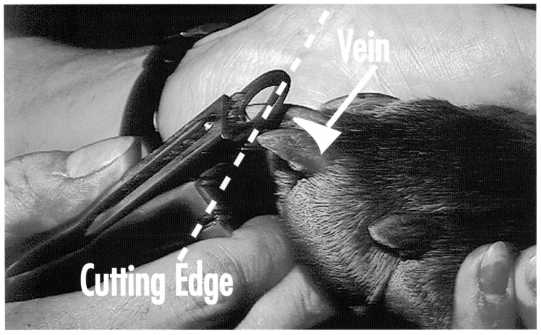

Vein

Cutting Edge

Avoid cutting the vein, or "quick."

cut the nail at a 45-degree angle. The cutting end of the nail clipper should be toward the end of the nail.

The frequency with which nails must be clipped depends on how much exercise your Weim gets on hard surfaces, like pavement.

If You Cut the Quick

If the worst happens and you nick the nail quick, keep some silver nitrate or a styptic pencil handy to stop the bleeding. You can get these items at your pet shop. Lacking these, you can use cornflour or flour. If the bleeding continues for more than 15 minutes, call your vet.

Drooling

Weimaraners are not natural droolers like Saint Bernards, so sudden drooling may indicate medical problems such as a cracked tooth, gum infection, obstruction in the throat, or even poisoning. Check your dog's mouth, and if the drooling continues, call your vet.

DENTAL CARE

Healthy gums and teeth are an important component of a healthy lifestyle. Dental disease is not only painful, but it can lead to kidney, liver, and respiratory infection as bacteria travel from the mouth through the bloodstream. Tooth and gum infections can weaken the facial bones and jaw, making your dog vulnerable to mandibular fractures and eye infections.

Bad teeth and infected gums cause eating problems, too. If you notice that your dog has trouble chewing kibble or seems to chew only on one side of the mouth, check his teeth. Bad breath, bleeding gums, or excessive drooling are signs that something is wrong. (Many dog food companies now offer "dental" food formulas; the idea is that the larger size kibble scrapes the teeth clean.) The most common cause of bad breath is tartar buildup around the teeth. (This goes for people, too.) If the tartar is allowed to accumulate, harmful bacteria may break loose and enter the dog's bloodstream, lodging in the internal organs. In fact, if you have an older dog with dirty teeth and a heart murmur, you have a good chance of clearing up the heart murmur just by cleaning the teeth. However, in older pets, it is possible that disease of the kidneys and liver can cause the dental problem.

Dental Disease

In the first stages of dental disease, plaque is just a yellowish, sticky coating on the teeth—most noticeable on the outside surface of the larger molars. It is made up of bacteria, saliva, food particles, and epithelial cells. Plaque builds up on the tooth surface and gum line *every day*. Left undisturbed, it will harden into calculus or tartar.

The buildup of tartar both above and below the gum line can eventually produce an environment that is a bacteria heaven. Eventually, periodontal disease results, affecting all the structures that support the teeth.

In severe cases, the gums are red or swollen. Additionally, as calculus builds up, the gums recede, exposing tooth enamel. Sometimes the bone around the teeth is lost faster than, or even without, gum loss. Periodontitis occurs in dogs of all ages and affects over 80 percent of dogs over three years of age. It is the leading cause of tooth loss.

Veterinary Cleaning

Once plaque sets in, your vet will need to give those teeth a thorough cleaning—under the gum line as well as above it. This is a procedure that requires general anaesthesia or heavy sedation because the noise and physical contact upset most dogs. The vet will use an ultrasonic scaler and then polish the teeth. The polishing isn't just for looks; it smooths the rough surfaces in the tooth enamel that food particles cling to. Although some people are terrified at the thought of subjecting an older dog to anaesthesia,

Healing Foot Infections

If your Weim's nails or paws have an infection (or are itchy from allergies), you can treat them with Epsom salts. Use 1/8 cup (.12 litres) per quart (.94 litres) of warm water and soak the paw for several minutes three times a day. This treatment will draw out the infection and relieve itchiness. Don't allow your dog to drink the salty water—it can produce diarrhoea.

Paws should be thoroughly dried after your dog returns from a romp in the wet outdoors; wet paws are targets for fungal infections.

Get the Right Chew Toys

Dogs who routinely chew on cages or hard plastic bones can fracture a tooth. This is just one more reason to provide your Weim with an appropriate selection of chew toys.

new anaesthetics are very safe—much safer than letting your dog struggle with gum disease.

If advanced periodontal disease has damaged the jawbone, the teeth may need to be removed. (In a few cases, several weeks of doxycycline therapy may save the teeth.) Some vets who specialise in dental work can even provide crowns for damaged dog teeth. This is usually just for cosmetic purposes, though.

Brushing

All dogs should be given yearly dental checkups, and most importantly, have their teeth brushed every day. Brushing your

Dental care is essential to your Weim's health.

Weim's teeth is an essential part of grooming and health care. While it is best to start when your dog is young, any time is better than never.

To accustom your dog to having his teeth brushed, start gradually by holding your Weim, lifting his lips, and checking his mouth. You can begin actual brushing by just rubbing a soft cloth across his teeth, then adding a special canine toothpaste (which come in flavours that your dog will like, such as chicken) and perhaps a rubber-tipped "massaging" brush that fits on your fingertip.

While dry food may retard the growth of plaque, only regular brushing will keep your Weim's teeth in excellent shape by reducing the amount of plaque and tartar that builds up. You also can buy doggy treats that may help to reduce tartar accumulation; check with your veterinarian about appropriate treats for your Weim. Because they aren't very digestible, I do not recommend rawhides.

Providing the right chew toys can prevent your Weim from damaging a tooth.

For more information about a home dental care regimen, contact your local veterinarian.

For the very best results, make regular dental appointments with your veterinarian.

While you are taking care of the teeth, be sure to notice irregularities in your Weim's mouth, such as swelling of the tongue or lips, bleeding from the mouth, abnormal gum colour, or excessive drooling. Report anything that seems amiss to your vet.

Mouthwash for Dogs

You can purchase chlorhexidine mouthwashes or sprays that contain enzymes to help to dissolve plaque. Using these produces is not as good as tooth brushing, but it's better than nothing.

C h a p t e r
6
TRAINING AND BEHAVIOUR
of Your Weimaraner

Dogs are not born knowing how to behave. Like children, they need to be taught. And if we don't teach them the way that we want them to behave, they will behave in a way that is natural to them. Some of what we call "undesirable behaviour" is, in fact, "natural" behaviour. Other undesirable behaviour on the dog's part is a result of undesirable behaviour on ours—leaving the animal alone too much, hitting him, screaming at him, or simply not clarifying for him what we'd like him to do.

In either case, much undesirable behaviour occurs because the owner is somehow failing to meet a dog's natural needs. The results can be disastrous. Objectionable pet behaviour has been found to be the main reason why people have poor relationships with their dogs. Eventually, many of these dogs are euthanised. Confused and frustrated owners often just give up, and their untrained dogs end up in animal shelters. Most of the problem is miscommunication. The owner sends the wrong message or a mixed message to the dog.

Never rush a young Weimaraner when it comes to training. This breed matures more slowly than other so-called "versatile" breeds. This is especially important if you ever dream of doing advanced work, like field trials. If your puppy does not seem to be performing to your expectations, the likelihood is that you have not completely trained the dog for those expectations.

FAMILY RULES

You and your family need to get together and decide as a group exactly what your dog will be permitted to do and what he won't. Weims are extremely clever at figuring out the weakest link and pushing their privileges with that person. Soon the rest of the family gives up trying to lay any ground rules at all, and the dog does what he wants. So decide together.

The entire family must decide what rules your Weim needs to follow.

- Will the dog be allowed to sleep on the sofa? On the bed?
- Will you let him beg for food?
- Will he be allowed to lick your face?
- What will be the rules for crating?

If you and your family can't decide what the rules are, your dog can't be expected to know either.

SOCIALISATION

Your Weim must get along with others. A well-socialised dog is a joy to bring with you when you travel and when you have guests. Lots of dogs obey their owners perfectly well—when they are in their homes. However, when they are out in the world, it can be a different story. The environment serves as a distraction. The more often your Weim gads about, the less distracting that things in the "outside world" will be for him.

Socialising a Puppy

Puppyhood, especially between the ages of 16 and 18 weeks of age, is the period of socialisation. Take advantage of it by making sure that your Weim has as many positive experiences with the world as possible. An isolated dog is a mistrustful dog. The more exposure he gets, the more trainable, stable, and sociable he will be. This is a solemn obligation on your part. The Weimaraner is not as

naturally social as a Beagle (although he's not a loner like a Chow Chow). He needs your encouragement to look at the world in an open, positive way.

Socialising your Weim doesn't mean that he won't still try to protect you. These dogs are naturally protective, but they should meet approved strangers with a friendly attitude. The best way to socialise your Weim is to take him out and about as much as possible. Different people, animals, and environments are your "socialisation targets." (However, make sure that any dogs he meets are fully vaccinated; your puppy is not fully protected until he is four months old.)

Your dog should experience without fear the following kinds of people: elderly or infirm people with canes, walkers, and wheelchairs; shouting people; timid people; joggers; bikers; people in uniforms and weird hats; babies; bearded people; and people of all races. He also should learn to handle different environments, including other people's homes, parks, lifts, stairs, and high-traffic areas (on a lead, of course).

Cats and Canines

If possible, try to socialise your dog to cats, although some Weims have a strong chase instinct. If that's the case, keep your dog away from cats. You can't change a prey drive.

Dog-to-Dog Relationships

It is very important that your Weim become accustomed to having friendly relationships with other dogs. Dogs are basically social creatures, after all, and they adapt well to a variety of living arrangements. But with dogs, oddly enough, sociability is connected with squabbling. If dogs were truly nonsocial, they would ignore each other. Instead, they form a "pack," and

Well-socialised puppies have been safely introduced to many different types of dogs, people, and things.

You're the Alpha Dog!

Many times a household of squabbling dogs is a good indication that the owner is weak or ineffectual. A strong leader simply exudes an atmosphere in which no fighting is permissible. In a few cases, however, a dog who was not properly socialised as a puppy will continue to have aggression problems, no matter how insightful the owner is.

often there is disagreement about who should lead it—hence the rumblings and sometimes outward fighting that is so abrasive to their owners.

Most serious fighting occurs between dogs of the same gender. In a normal household, fighting is most likely to occur when the previous "top dog" ages or the younger dog suddenly "comes into his own," usually between the time is he is 18 months to 3 years of age. It's especially noticeable when one of the contenders has been absent for a period of time. (In my house, the period of absence can be an hour.) Although nerve-wracking, this kind of squabbling is seldom serious, as long as you do not try to "make things right" by deciding who you think should be leader. Let the dogs sort it out for themselves. If you intervene, the squabbling will get worse and last longer.

The solution in some cases is as simple as neutering the offending male. More commonly, the owner needs to take firm hold as a leader and attempt to figure out what kinds of situations prompt the violence. If it's food, don't allow the dogs to eat near each other. Put them in separate rooms if you have to. If you give treats, give easy-to-swallow ones, not rawhide bones or other things that become "possessions." Some dogs fight when they enter enclosed spaces. If this is the case with your dogs, teach them to "wait" before allowing them to plunge out the door at the same time and start fighting. All dogs should know basic obedience commands.

Enhance the position of the naturally dominant dog by feeding, petting, greeting, and walking him first. The lower ranked dog will soon figure out that he has no allies in his quest for leadership and will settle down into second place. You must do this even if you like the lower status dog best. If frequent fights occur, make sure that the dogs are wearing a harness or some other suitable neckwear so that you can easily grab them. Don't stick your hand into a dogfight—you know what will happen.

In extremely serious cases, you may have to separate the dogs temporarily or permanently. In some cases, pharmaceutical intervention may help, but that should be a last resort.

MAINTAINING YOUR LEADERSHIP

Weimaraners are the most loving of dogs, but they are not weak, submissive softies. Unless you decide to be the leader, your dog

will take over the job. As social animals, dogs know that good behaviour comes from good social structure.

The reason that owners don't have more problems than they do is that dogs are amazingly adaptable. Many dogs seem to think "Hmmm….what a strange grouping. No discernible leader….. hmmm. Well, I'll just go along with it for now." And often, that's an end to it. But strongly dominant dogs—and Weims tend in this direction—may think "Hmmm…what a bunch of losers. Sweet, but no clue, really. No leader. I presume, therefore, that the position is vacant." And they step in, not because they passionately want to be the leader but because they expect *someone* to be the leader.

Humans encourage this behaviour when they don't give their dogs any structure or discipline and when they treat their dogs as equals. They don't make rules, don't enforce them, or enforce them erratically. Dogs understand very well that the sofa is more comfortable than the floor, that your food is a welcome addition to theirs, and that being bossy often gets them what they want. They put this strategy into play whenever they think that they can get away with it. The dog may even try the old canine trick of growling to express displeasure at being moved or at having his territory encroached upon. This applies to personal territory like his face, food bowl, bed, or toy. If the owner does not properly respond to the growl, the next step may be a bite. The dog does not feel that biting is "wrong." He feels that it's a tool he can use when he feels stressed.

In the vast majority of cases, dogs attempt to wrest leadership from children and others whom they perceive as weak. To prevent this from happening, you need to be strong—not cruel or bullying,

To Diffuse a Scuffle

If you see a fight coming on, it may help to distract one of the dogs by playing a game that requires concentration. Luckily, dogs can think about only one thing at a time.

It's important to be a strong, positive leader with your Weim.

Sources of Aggression

While many types of aggression exist, all except prey drive are in response to some stressor, which is some factor that threatens the dog's sense of well-being.

but just in charge of things. I have yet to see a dog take over leadership from a strong person. Your dog reads your leadership competence by your stance, voice, and confidence. A good leader speaks firmly. She stands tall and doesn't use kitchy-coo baby talk to a dominant dog. Also, she does not scream or resort to physical violence that merely masks incompetence.

If your dog has already assumed alpha status, things will be tougher. Your dog is now used to being the boss and likes it. Obviously, you shouldn't simply attack him the way a wolf might attack a rival. And if your dog has serious aggression problems—meaning that he has bitten a human being—you need to contact a professional immediately.

If things haven't progressed that far, you may be able to handle things yourself, as long as you are willing to be consistent and strong and not let yourself get lulled into the "Oh, he didn't mean it, I know he loves me" syndrome.

The way to restore the proper balance in your household is to simply be the boss. From this day forward, you decide where he sleeps, for example, which will *not* be in your bed or on your furniture. In fact, keep him out of your bedroom. That's your den, and he has to earn the right to be there. Put him in his crate to sleep.

You also decide what and when he eats and when and how long he will be exercised. It's hard to overdo exercise with a Weim, and your first step toward recovery should be long and exhaustive exercise. Bike riding with your dog on a lead is great for this kind of thing—plenty of running for him and plenty of control for you. The more tired he is, the happier and less stressed he is and the less time he has to think about taking over. This is not as hard as it seems. Dogs really have only a few ways of "taking over," and they can all be solved.

Monitoring Aggression

It is helpful to keep a journal with an aggressive dog. For each incident, write down:

- what the aggression consisted of (snap, growl, snarl, bite, or whatever)
- what triggered it
- to whom it was directed toward

By keeping track of when your dog becomes aggressive, you'll be better able to avoid the circumstances, to retrain your dog, and to assist in working with a professional.

You will no longer coddle or cuddle your dog. That's right. As emotionally satisfying as it may be to curl up with your pooch, that time has passed with a dominant dog. Be friendly but distant. If he nudges you for affection, walk away.

If your dog is possession-aggressive, don't give him any treat that he cannot eat in a second or two, and if he's food-aggressive, start feeding him by hand, piece by piece. (This point is to make him realise that all food comes from you and that he can't hog it.) If he is protective of his bed, make him sleep on the floor. If he refuses to get off the sofa even after a firm command, tip the sofa so that he has to get off.

Aggressive Games

Aggressive games like tug-of-war should cease immediately and forever with dogs who want to take over things.

Do routine obedience with him every day. The *sit, lie down,* and *stay* cues are minimum requirements. Make him perform for his supper, and use a strong voice. Don't be too lavish with the praise; just let him know that this is what you expect of him. If you never taught him to sit, do so now. (See section on teaching the *sit* in the "Working With Weimaraners" section.) If he knows how to sit but refuses, walk away and ignore him. Weims are such attention seekers that he'll soon learn to obey.

If you find your Weim challenging your leadership position, you may want to consult with a trainer or behaviourist for help.

Occasionally, the problem is only with certain members of the family, usually children or others whom the dog perceives as being underlings. These are the very ones who should feed, exercise, and work with the dog to command his obedience. The rule should be that all human beings are "alpha" to all dogs. Dogs are programmed to live in a dominance hierarchy, so it's up to you to establish which members of the group are going to be on top. None of them should have four legs.

Even if treatment is successful, there's never a guarantee that aggressive behaviour will not return with future stress. Your best chance of avoiding it is to make sure that the triggers are "locked." Any dog who has shown aggression must at the very least be kept away from children and visitors.

HOUSETRAINING

Weimaraners have an unfortunate reputation in some quarters of being slow to housetrain. This is due, in part, to the fact that the breed is slow to mature. In other cases, owners just haven't been patient or clever enough.

While several valid approaches to housetraining exist, the basic rules for all of them are the same: stay calm, be patient, and don't hit or yell. Praise your puppy when he does the right thing. And if your puppy has an accident and you notice it after it has occurred, don't yell at him or stick his face in it. He won't remember what he did wrong and so won't understand why you are chastising him.

Using the Crate

Today, the popular method of housetraining a dog is "crate training." Because dogs don't like soiling their beds, the theory is that confining them to a small area will encourage them to "hold it."

The crate should be just roomy enough for your dog to lie down, stand up, and turn around in. A crate that is too big will allow your puppy simply to move to the other side to urinate or defecate and rest comfortably in another spot. If you have a puppy, you can buy a crate that comes with a divider panel. This will allow you to adjust the position of the panel as your puppy grows. Put the crate in a quiet but not isolated area. Avoid high-traffic places like the kitchen.

Proper Cleanup for Housetraining Accidents

If your dog has a housetraining accident, it's important to remove all traces of the urine. If you don't, your dog will be tempted to return to the same spot. If it's fresh urine, clean the rug with a good carpet shampoo. However, if the urine has penetrated through the rug to the pad beneath, it's unlikely that you'll be able to remove it completely. Good odour removers are products that contain enzymes to break down the odour-causing compounds in urine and faeces. Follow the directions carefully, and let the cleaner soak in as deeply as the urine itself. You will have to keep the spot warm and wet for 24 hours. It helps to cover the area with plastic.

If the urine has soaked into unsealed concrete, you will have to neutralise the urine and then seal the concrete. You may need professional help for this.

For hardwood floors, use an enzymatic product to remove the odour. In some cases, you'll need to remove the varnish or polyurethane from the area and sand it. You may wish to consult a professional before you do something as complicated as this.

Never punish your puppy for housetraining mistakes.

Most dogs readily accept the idea of a crate; if yours doesn't, you may have to lure him in with treats. Never force your dog into a crate or use it for punishment because that will do more harm than good. You need to convince him that a crate is a great place to be. Give him a special command at the same time, such as "naptime" or anything else that you choose. Soon he'll associate your command with going in his "den."

For an adult dog who is unused to the crate, be patient. Try feeding him in the crate, and don't shut the door on him. Start slowly by shutting the door for a few seconds, and then gradually increase the time that the door remains closed. You also can start leaving the room for very brief periods.

However, keeping a young dog in a crate for more than an hour or two can be stressful. Weimaraners are highly energetic dogs who need physical and mental stimulation. Restrict the use of a crate to times when you cannot watch your dog, and never leave him in there for extended period of time except at night when he is sleeping. And be sure to walk him right before and immediately after "crate time."

Be Consistent

Prepare your puppy for what is to happen by giving him a verbal cue "Bathroom!" or "Outside!" in a happy, excited tone. Use the same command every time. Some people use a urine-soaked

Submissive Urination

One type of inappropriate urination is submissive urination, a behaviour that a frightened dog uses to show deference to a dominant creature (possibly yourself). Ignoring this behaviour usually will result in its disappearance. Under no circumstance should you punish a dog for doing it. It will only get worse.

cloth as a cue that their dog is to urinate in that spot. However, the idea of carrying a urine-soaked cloth around isn't all that appealing.

When you take your dog outside for a potty break, watch him carefully. Take him on a lead to the same spot every time. When he does what is required, praise him extravagantly. (Weims are suckers for flattery.) What follows next is a matter of some controversy. Some trainers believe that you should immediately take the dog back in the house so that he will learn that the purpose of the potty break is just that and should not be confused with playtime. They theorise that if it turns into playtime, the dog will not understand why he is out there. Other trainers believe that if a dog is immediately removed from the interesting outdoors the minute he urinates or defecates, he'll prolong it as much as possible to enjoy himself as long as possible. A sensible compromise can be reached. Watch your puppy and do not play with him until he has succeeded. You can then play with him briefly as a reward before going back inside. Of course, you'll have a longer playtime later.

You can help housetraining go more smoothly by feeding your puppy on a consistent schedule. Some dogs seem to want to "go" right after eating—for others it's half an hour or more. This is not something that the puppy can control. Find out how your dog's toileting system works, and work with it. If you are not regular with his feeding, he won't be regular with his toileting. It's as simple as that. Active playing or drinking a lot of water also can trigger toileting in a puppy.

Sometimes urination occurs when the puppy is excited because his sphincter control is not yet perfect. Don't bother correcting this behaviour—he can't help it, but he will grow out of it. Just wipe it up without comment. Frightened pups also may urinate—again,

Puppy Mistakes

If your puppy makes a mistake in the house, don't correct him unless it happens right in front your eyes. For a dog, all past is long past. He'll have no idea what you are talking about. Besides, there's no doubt that your clever Weimaraner was giving you clues that you may have missed—looking at the door, walking in circles, or licking his nose.

Instead of responding with anger, simply pick your puppy up and say "Outside!" Then, take him there. Push his tail down as you go—this may delay the inevitable until you are safe outside. Never send your dog outside alone—go with him and be ready to praise.

Most dogs give a pre-toileting signal. These signals vary from dog to dog but are pretty consistent for an individual. Once you learn your pup's "toileting language," you're on your way!

don't react to it—just clean it up. When he grows more confident, the behaviour will stop, almost certainly before he is one year old. Rescue or shelter dogs may take a little longer. If you can install one, a doggy door may be helpful here.

WORKING WITH WEIMARANERS

The same high drive and energy that makes the Weimaraner such a superb hunter

Patience and consistency are key when housetraining your Weim.

can be distracting when he is bouncing, leaping, and jumping around the house. This is part of the Weim's nature; he'll slow down as he ages, but young dogs are gifted with this incredible store of energy that they must work off one way or another. Some of it can be directed toward training, but you're wiser if you take your dog for a good run before beginning a training session so that he'll settle down (somewhat) and listen to you.

Watch Me

It's helpful to train your dog a little bit every day. It not only reinforces what he knows, but it also helps to relieve boredom and improves communication between the two of you. To this end, one of the first things that your Weim should learn is *watch me*. This means "Make eye contact with me right now and keep looking. Don't pay any attention to anything else." Dogs are pretty good watchers, but training your pet to make and understand eye contact is immensely helpful. It helps to calm a nervous dog and can help to prevent an aggressive dog from going after another animal.

At first you may need to say "Watch me" and move your head a bit. Reward your dog with a treat as he follows your motion. Soon he'll be watching you pretty much all the time, and you can reward with a treat only occasionally.

Getting Started

- First, decide exactly what the goal of the training

One of the first things your Weim should learn is the "Watch me" command.

session is going to be. If you don't know, your dog certainly won't. Make the goal attainable within a few minutes. This means that complicated commands may have to be broken up into "bits" over several days. A good rule for a puppy is that training sessions should last about ten minutes and should be undertaken three times a day. Any longer will bore or stress the puppy.

- Before you begin, have all the treats (good, soft, high-value ones, not just a bit of dog biscuit). The treats should go into a readily retrievable pouch or pocket.
- Pick a quiet indoor place (there are too many distractions outside) and a time when your dog is hungry but not starving. As mentioned earlier, it also helps to exercise the Weim first so that he works off some of that extraneous energy.
- The first rule is that there should be only one trainer and only one dog. It's impossible to train two dogs at the same time (the distraction is unbearable for everyone), and the dog will learn better if he has to pay attention only to you.
- Always end the training on a successful note, even if you have to repeat something that your dog already knows. Be assured that if he is not "getting it," either you are doing something completely wrong or you are trying to teach him to do something impossible, such as calculus.

Blueprint for Success

Start the training with a brief review of something that your dog already understands, and praise him for succeeding. Don't yell at him or wag your finger in his face. This will only upset or frighten him. Most successful training takes place in several steps:

- Get your dog to do the behaviour (usually with a treat or some other lure).
- Command the behaviour, such as "Sit!" as he does it.
- Practice that a while.
- Reduce the treat factor, changing to praise for success.
- Make the exercise more challenging by increasing length, distance, duration, or whatever.
- Add distractions.
- End the training session on a positive, successful note. At your

next training session, work on something different. Keep it interesting.

TEACHING BASIC OBEDIENCE COMMANDS

In your early training sessions, you'll work solely on teaching simple obedience commands. It is critical that your dog respond to commands, particularly the *come* cue.

Come or Here

To teach your Weim to come to you, start with him on a rope 18 to 20 ft. (5.5 to 6 m) in length. Let him wander off, then call him to you while saying the command in an excited, happy voice: "Here, here, here!" or "Come, come, come!" If he comes, give him a small treat or some affection; if he doesn't come, gently pull him to you and reward him when he gets to you. Drill him over and over.

Many Weims respond better to a whistle than to voice or hand commands. Get yourself a stainless steel "referee" whistle with a lanyard attached. The classic whistle command to teach a Weimaraner the *come* cue is three sharp blows on the whistle. This is a very loud sound that can carry quite far in Autumn and winter.

To train your Weim to come using a whistle, start in a small area and bring your bag of treats. Sit right down in front of him, blow the whistle three times softly, and then hand over a treat. (This is basically the same method as clicker training, but Weims can outrun the sound of a clicker pretty quickly.) Do this a few times, and then go play. Repeat the drill a few hours later, and stand farther away from him. Soon he'll associate the sound of the whistle with you, petting, and treats. A word of warning—this will not work if your Weimaraner has found game. Nothing will.

If you are training outside, keep your puppy on a lead.

Leave It!

The *leave it* cue is also a lifesaver. Dogs are forever getting into rubbish and poison, not to mention your own dinner. Start teaching your Weim to leave it by waiting until he is chewing on an object that he really doesn't care *that*

A long lead or retractable lead can help when teaching come.

much about. (It also should be one that's not important to you, either, of course.) As he's chewing, go up to him and say "Leave it!" Offer him a treat in exchange. Practice several times a day, and always offer him a treat that he likes (like bacon) better than whatever he is chewing. You want to reinforce that he'll be richly rewarded, not given a mere sop like a dog biscuit.

In real life, you will be most likely to use this command when your dog has gotten into something truly heady, like a chicken carcass, so your established reward needs to be very powerful. Of course, you probably won't have any bacon actually on hand when the chicken carcass event occurs, but it's okay to cheat that one time and just reward him with a biscuit. Afterward, practice the *leave it* command several more times with your accustomed treat and plenty of praise.

Lie Down

Teach *lie down* after *sit*. (See section on *sit*.) At that point, you have the rear half down, at least. The hard part is the front half. Most dogs dislike being asked to lie down, although they are happy enough to do it on their own. This is because *lie down* puts them in a physically and psychologically vulnerable position.

Use the treat method again. While your dog is sitting, lower it slowly and move it toward the floor. Most dogs will lie down naturally. If yours doesn't after a few tries, you can gently extend his front legs and praise him as you ease him to the floor.

Don't push down on your Weimaraner's shoulders to force him down; you can actually dislocate his shoulder in trying to coerce him. Besides, you already know you're stronger than he is. You want him to perform joyfully, not out of fear or pain.

As your Weimaraner becomes an expert at following commands while you are standing by, gradually increase the distance between yourself and your dog. One additional step away a day is far enough.

Off!

It's a funny thing about Weimaraners. They tend to always be *on* what you want them *off.* The answer is not necessarily disallowing the privilege of furniture but teaching them a positive rather than a negative command.

To teach this cue, say "Off!" in a cheerful voice. Of course, if you never want your dog on that piece of furniture, you can use your dark growly voice, but if you just want to move him temporarily, the *off* command works very well. *Off* also works nicely when you want your Weimaraner to jump out of the car. In fact, your dog should only leave the car when you command him to.

Sit

Sit is an easy command to teach, but it is often used inappropriately—usually when the owner really wants her dog to stay still, get out of the way, or not make a nuisance of himself. The catchall "Sit, boy" is supposed to magically cure all the bad habits

Be patient when teaching the Down command—many dogs dislike this position.

95

your dog has gotten himself into. It doesn't, of course, and it's much better to work on actually curing your dog's bad habits (like jumping up) than to tell him to sit every time that he does them. Think of it this way. Most of the time, when you ask your dog to sit, you really would be happy if he just stood there quietly. If that's what you want, that's what you must teach him. *Sit* is a useful command, of course. I ask my dogs to sit before I give them a treat because it's easier for me to find their little mouths that way. It's also useful as a prelude to nail clipping, and it's a simple trick for children to practice with the family dog. But it's no substitute for good all-around behaviour.

The easiest way to teach this cue is to say "Sit" in a cheerful voice while holding a treat over your Weim's head. Start gently curving the treat backward over his head. Most dogs will

Sit is on of the easiest commands to teach your puppy.

sit naturally. Praise him and give him the treat. Never *force* him—encourage him. Nothing about the training should be uncomfortable. Praise him softly, and while he is still sitting, give him a treat. If he gets up too quickly, refrain from giving the treat. He needs to learn that the treat comes only when he is actually sitting. Otherwise, you'll turn him into a jack-in-the-box.

Wait

Wait is a nice, calming command, useful when you have company. Your dog doesn't have to sit, which can be very trying when friends have arrived; instead, he must merely stand quietly and wait to be petted. It's also useful for keeping your dog from charging for the door while you open it—either to let someone in or to go out yourself.

To teach the *wait* command, begin by attaching a short lead to your Weim. This will serve to give you a little control. Touch him quietly on the rump and say "Wait" when a visitor arrives. Use the lead to restrain him if you have to, and reward him for quietly waiting to be petted.

Whoa!

This emergency field command is a lifesaver. Its purpose is to get your Weimaraner to stop immediately. It is most useful when he has escaped from the house and is headed directly into the street. Calling "Come" might tell your Weimaraner that you want him home, but he's apt to make a large circle while doing so—right into the traffic. *Whoa* tells him to stop at once. Once he stops in his tracks, you can walk over to him and snap on his lead.

To begin teaching this cue, you need a plain collar (not a choke chain), a lead, and a flexi-lead. Start with the regular lead. While he is standing still (as you want him to), say "Whoa!" Then praise him or give him a treat, but keep him standing. After a short period of praise, say "Release!" and play (but don't run) with him. Then try again. Soon he should associate "Whoa!" with standing still and receiving a treat. As time goes on, use the flexi-lead instead of the regular lead. This allows you more distance but still helps you to maintain control. If your dog doesn't respond to "Whoa!", stop him with the lead. When he stops, praise him and give him a treat, or play with him some more. It's very important that his reward is not a run. You want to connect the whole procedure of "stopping and

Training Your Weim to "Bow"

This is an impressive trick that's pretty easy to teach. Put a high-value food treat beneath your standing Weim. As he starts to "bow" to get it, say "Bow!" If he manages to get the treat without bowing, you will have to hold it in your fist but in the same place. It's a bit awkward, but it will work. Either way, praise your dog (or use a clicker if you are clicker training) when he bows. Repeat several times, and pretty soon he will bow on command.

staying" with praise and food. When he "whoas" reliably on lead, you can try him off lead. Use your garden or some other boring, fenced area for starters.

If you have done a good, thorough job with *whoa*, you just might save your Weimaraner's life. You can never absolutely count on your dog's obedience, however, so even with an apparently completely obedient Weimaraner, it's not wise to allow him off lead in the hopes that this command will automatically save him if he runs into traffic.

Walk Nicely (Heel)

Your lead is your dog's best friend. Don't think of the lead as a restraining device; think of it as a way to stay close to your dog. With only a little encouragement, your Weimaraner will look forward happily to the sight of the lead being taken off its hook; it means walk time!

Before you start lead training your Weimaraner, give him a lot of free exercise. A somewhat tired dog will be more amenable to moving at a slow pace.

Reward your puppy with a small treat when he performs the desired behaviour.

Weimaraners like to go first. Remember that they are bred to be leaders on a hunt. To some extent, you are working against Weimaraner nature when you are asking him to follow you. You must replace his natural hunting instinct with an equally natural instinct of "follow the leader." When he becomes convinced that *you* are the leader and that you know where the "pack" is supposed to go, he'll be more eager to follow (unless he scents a rabbit and you don't). So walk fast, at least at first. Walking quickly keeps his attention directed straight ahead, where you want it while training.

Begin teaching your Weimaraner to heel once he has mastered the *come* command. Enforce your command to heel, if necessary, by kneeling and using a treat to lure him. Don't pull on the lead. Only use it to keep him from going in the other direction.

Lead control comes in handy when you are out for walks and potty breaks.

It's customary to have your dog walk on your left side, so if you plan to engage in formal obedience training, you might as well start developing the correct practice right away. Start by keeping a little treat in your left hand. The point is to get your Weimaraner to believe that staying close to that appendage is likely to yield its rewards. Give your dog a treat frequently as you walk along but only when he's in the correct *heel* position. To help position your dog, hold the lead behind your thigh. Start walking in a circle in a counterclockwise direction. Because your dog will be on the inside, you'll find it easier to guide him as you move along. Say "Roxy, heel!" in a bright voice and start walking. Don't scold him if he goes in the wrong direction—just don't respond to it. Stay still or move in a different way. Soon he'll realise that all the rewards come from staying near you.

After your Weimaraner becomes accustomed to walking on the lead and you don't have to give him a treat every two seconds for walking politely, ask him to sit when you stop, and reward him when he does. Soon your Weimaraner will sit calmly by your side whenever you stop to chat with friends. If you do not want your Weimaraner to sit automatically at every stop, make sure that you say "Sit" before you give him a treat.

Clicker Training

One popular form of positive training is "clicker training," invented many years ago by psychologists Breland and Breland and then forgotten. It was "reinvented" by dolphin trainers (using a whistle) and then applied to zoo animals and finally to dogs.

This method uses a small plastic device with a button that makes a loud clicking sound. Clicker training precisely marks a behaviour, so your dog knows exactly what you are rewarding him for.

Don't make every walk a lesson. Allow your Weimaraner plenty of time to snoop around and check things out, especially when you begin your walk. It may be exasperating to you, but Weimaraners really enjoy this part of the adventure. You can signal to your Weimaraner that it is his turn to lead at a certain part of the walk by using some special command (whatever you like) and loosening up on the lead. I say, "You lead!" and start following him. This is very important if you plan to do tracking with your Weimaraner.

For inveterate pullers, or if you have untrustworthy small children, purchase the Wayne Hightower harness, which simply has the loop in the front of the harness at chest level rather than at the back. It is simple, dogs love it, and it works better than anything else I have seen, including head halters.

FINDING A PROFESSIONAL TRAINER

Many kinds of training are available for your Weim. (You needn't wait for a problem to occur before you seek the help of a pro.) I recommend enrolling your Weimaraner early in dog training classes, which teach socialisation as well as obedience.

Obedience training teaches many of the fundamentals discussed earlier: *come, sit, stay, down, off,* and *heel.* More advanced work may include fetch and the basics to begin work in agility or competitive obedience. Another kind of training often is sought to help modify a dog's problem behaviour. Some trainers offer private lessons and will come to your home; others use a group setting to encourage socialisation. This is particularly important for puppies.

To find a good basic obedience class, check with your vet, local rescue centre, or breed club for a recommendation. You also can check with the Association of Pet Dog Trainers (APDT) on the Internet (www.apdt.co.uk) for local approved trainers. The APDT is an educational organisation dedicated to promoting humane training methods. Its members use reinforcements and positive training rather than coercive, intimidating, or punishment-based training techniques.

Whenever possible, visit a class before you enroll your dog. (Good obedience classes require that your dog be vaccinated before lessons begin.) Ask what professional organisations the instructor belongs to. Observe how the instructor(s) interacts with the dogs and their owners. The dogs should seem happy and fearless. The instructor should be able to explain herself clearly and should be able to demonstrate the behaviour that she wants her students to learn. If she loses her temper or uses hurtful means to accomplish the training, leave. This class is not for you.

PROBLEM BEHAVIOURS

It's important to remember that most problem behaviours, such as jumping up, barking, resource guarding, sexual behaviour, protecting territory, chewing, and nipping, are all natural dog behaviours. They become a problem for owners when they are inconvenient and interfere with what we like.

Changing problem behaviours into acceptable behaviours involves understanding canine body language, socialising the dog, and giving him plenty of positive things to do. And it is always easier to prevent an unwanted behaviour than to deal with it afterward.

Attention-Seeking Behaviour

People-oriented dogs like Weims adore your attention, and some will go to almost any length to get it. At first it's cute and even flattering—later, however, it can become a real nuisance. Attention-seeking behaviour ranges from a gentle but insistent nudge to loud barking and jumping in your face. (Never underestimate just how

Some problem behaviours have an underlying medical cause, so see your vet first.

Drug Treatment

Some problem behaviours can be managed with pharmaceuticals. However, because most drugs are metabolised through the liver and kidneys, these functions must be evaluated before and during treatment. In addition, many medications have side effects. For example, fluoxetine (Prozac), while useful in addressing certain unwanted behaviours, causes gastrointestinal problems and restlessness in some animals. Drug therapy works best when used in combination with training.

high a Weim can jump.) Some paw at you. Some will steal anything you're holding. A few have been known to roll around on the floor, apparently in agony, to get you to pay attention to their feigned ailment. Others have been known to actually vomit.

Because your Weim is engaging in this behaviour to get your attention, any kind of attention he gets for it (including negative attention) is a reward for him. To cure the problem, you'll have to ignore your dog—consistently ignore him when he seeks attention. (However, be sure that you *do* give him attention when he is quiet and undemanding. Dogs do need attention, and Weimaraners in particular thrive on it.) This is harder than it seems because at first the problem will get worse, not better, as your dog intensifies his attempts to make you pay attention. He'll just figure that because his previous attempts have been unsuccessful, he needs to try a little harder. After an undetermined period, however, your intelligent Weim will decide that his tactics no longer work.

Some behaviourists suggest using a so-called "bridging" device to hasten progress. With this plan, whenever your dog engages in the unwanted behaviour, you blow a whistle or use some other signal to let him know in advance what you are about to do: leave the room. The bridging device helps to focus the dog's attention on precisely what he's doing the second before you leave. This in turn leads to a quicker discontinuance of the behaviour.

Barking (Nuisance)

Dogs bark. It's a normal part of their behaviour. They bark to alert us to visitors, they bark in play, and they bark when they want something. It is not possible or desirable to eliminate all barking in our canine friends. However, sometimes barking exceeds tolerable limits. In that case, it's called "nuisance barking."

Nuisance barking can be a serious problem in Weimaraners, but it almost always occurs in dogs who are left alone for long periods. Unlike terriers, Shelties, and many smaller breeds, the Weim is not genetically "programmed" to be a barker—but a lonely situation can quickly turn him into one. And it is true that some Weims seem to enjoy listening to themselves bark. This is sometimes known as recreational barking.

Alarm Barking

However, the Weim can be an "alarm" barker—letting you know

when you have visitors of any species. This isn't a bad thing—you want your dog to do his job. The problem begins when you can't shut the alarm off or when he barks for another reason, such as to guard his territory or to express his boredom and despair. For the territorial barker, it may help to obscure the boundary beyond your house and your neighbour's house by installing stockade-type fencing. Chain link allows a dog to see what's going on next door and pay far too much attention to it.

Exercise is Key

Lots and lots of exercise can help curb attention-seeking behaviour.

If you hear your dog barking outside, bring him in immediately. That may be what he wants anyway, and who can blame him? Standing around all by oneself in the garden isn't all that much fun. Most importantly, however, it may annoy the neighbours. And you don't want that. In my hometown, a local science teacher was convicted of actually poisoning the dog next door because his barking annoyed him. While I am quite sure that your neighbours are not like this, you never really know.

If your Weim is barking while he is standing right next to you, slide your hand under his collar at the back of his neck. Pull up slightly to immobilise his head, and with the other hand, press down on his muzzle and say "Quiet," in a low, dark, firm voice. Be calm. Repeat until your dog gets the idea.

Boredom and Neurotic Barking

Your Weim may be barking because he's bored. The cure is simple (but not always easy)—exercise! Healthy young Weimaraners need more exercise than almost any other breed—at least two hours of it every day, and I

An organised sport like agility can keep your Weim's body and mind occupied, and help alleviate some problem behaviours.

don't mean a casual walk. You may need to hire someone to play, jog, or swim with your dog, but it will be worth it. At the very least, try to give him a run before you go to work and after you come home. Don't be surprised, though, if that is not enough.

Closely related to this is the neurotic barker. Boredom does lead to neurosis and separation anxiety. Again, the cure lies in more training, work, play, and sensible, disciplined treatment. In

serious cases, medication may be needed, at least temporarily.

To minimise barking while you are gone, keep your dog in a quiet part of your home, draw the blinds (darkness is calming), and leave the radio on, tuned to a talk station. This white noise masks other noises and comforts your dog with the sound of a human voice.

Begging

Begging is a behaviour that is partly natural and partly learned. Most of the time, it is not serious and can even be cute—until your 70-pound (32 kg) Weim escalates mournful looks into whining, barking, pawing, nuzzling, or just plain grabbing. (It's a mistake to think that begging applies only to food. Your Weim also might beg to play, get a seat on the sofa, or be handed a favourite toy.)

You're best off if you never reward begging in the first place, because prevention is always easier than cures. To do this, you must vow to *never* feed your dog from the table or respond to

Try to resist that pleading look—it only leads to constant begging!

pleading looks. If you respond just once, you're sunk. And you've already done that, haven't you? (Join the club.) Dogs beg simply because begging has worked in the past, and they feel confident that it will work again in the future.

If you've already inadvertently rewarded begging, what you can do now is to resolve to never again reward this behaviour. You can achieve some success by feeding and exercising your dog on a set schedule. Dogs like to know when to expect things; it reduces their anxiety and therefore their need to beg. If possible, feed your Weim at the same time but in a separate place (maybe his crate) from where you eat yourself.

Don't punish your dog for begging, but don't reward him either. And don't expect it to stop after a day or two. Your dog will keep trying for a quite a while. Be strong.

Use *Take It*

If you ever feed your dog by hand, give him a specific command such as *take it* before you offer it to him. Keep your fist closed on the treat. Give it to him on *your* incentive, not on his initiative.

Chewing (Inappropriate)

Dogs have teeth, strong, powerful teeth meant for ripping and tearing game. For the contemporary Weimaraner, that game often may be the living room sofa, your grandmother's quilt, or your Gucci shoes.

Young dogs chew because they're curious, lonely dogs chew because they're bored, and frightened dogs chew to calm themselves down. The results are the same in each case, but knowing the cause will help you deal with the situation.

The Curious Chewer

Curious chewers explore their world with their teeth. Anything is fair game—the television remote, your thesis, and that hideous doily Aunt Hildegarde tatted up sometime during the last century. (You're probably just as happy that it's gone, but don't let your Weimaraner know it.) Some experts think that teething dogs are especially prone to chewing either because their gums feel irritated or because in some way we don't understand that chewing actually helps "set the teeth." In either case, we do know that it's natural.

For this kind of chewing, the answer is easy—supervised chewing of appropriate objects. *You* decide what is appropriate. This can safely be done inside a crate as long as you are not imprisoning your dog in the crate but merely offering him a good private place to get in some serious chewing.

For longer periods, use a kitchen or bathroom as an extended "crate," carefully putting all tempting items out of reach. Tempting items to a dog go far beyond what you might consider ingestible. They include razors, hearing aids, watches, glasses, and magazines.

Weimaraners, along with most other sporting breeds, do not stop chewing simply because they have reached technical "adulthood." Most will chew voraciously until they are at least two years old.

The Lonely Chewer

Inappropriate chewing may be the number-one problem that Weimaraner owners face. But it's not surprising. Sadly, it's not uncommon for a dog in our culture to be left alone for 10 to 12 hours every day. Because dogs are bred to require human companionship, these long, lonely hours can seem unbearable to many dogs, including Weimaraners, who seem especially devoted and dependent upon their human family.

If this sounds like your dog, please don't scold or yell at him for doing the only thing he can think of to relieve his boredom and stress. Keep in mind that it's not fair to lock him up in a crate without mental and physical stimulation for hours at a time.

If the chewing is connected with a longing for companionship, your best option (assuming you can't quit your job and stay home with him all day) is to ask a friend (or hire a dog walker) to walk your dog or play with him. The money it costs is more than made up for in a happier dog and fewer destroyed household items.

Some destructive chewing can be a sign of boredom.

You also should provide good, interesting toys for your dog while you're gone and leave on the radio. (Talk radio is preferable.) It's tempting but not necessarily a good idea to get a second dog, especially if you don't have sufficient time for the first one.

The Stressed Chewer

Dogs also chew to relieve stress, whether that stress is caused by boredom, fear, or anxiety. The stressed chewer typically chews on personal objects—yours. The items appear to give a sense of comfort, but when your underwear is not available, the dog will chew anything within reach (and something that you had no idea that he could possibly reach).

To address the problem, you'll need to sort out the cause of the stress and then attempt to deal with it.

Luckily, your vet can prescribe a temporary anti-anxiety medication, which along with a behavioural modification programme, will work wonders in restoring your dog to sanity and your house to order.

Loneliness

It is tempting to get a second dog to try and help alleviate loneliness in your Weim. However, if you don't have time for one dog, it's not a good idea to add another.

Coprophagia

Coprophagia is a fancy name for stool eating. It's actually a rather normal behaviour. Mother dogs eat their puppies' faeces to keep the area clean, and young dogs tend to eat everything that comes in their path, whether it's technically food or not. Most dogs eventually grow out of this unwholesome habit, but some do not. Some eat only their own faeces, while others prefer the leavings of other dogs. Many can't resist cat faeces, and a few eat only frozen-solid faeces that they find around the garden in the winter. No one knows exactly why this behaviour occurs, although a number of theories have been advanced, including not enough mental and physical exercise and poor food.

Various home remedies have been suggested, but most of them really don't work very well. Your best strategy is to pick up in your garden every day so that your Weim doesn't have the chance to indulge in this distasteful hobby. In some cases, a high-fibre diet has been found to help both with dogs who ate their own stool and with dogs who ate that of other dogs. No one really knows why. Giving your dog plenty of exercise is also beneficial—remember that a tired Weim is a well-behaved Weim. In a few cases, anti-obsessional drugs have brought positive results.

If your dog appropriates the sofa when you're not at home, against orders, you may need to resort to management such as putting clear plastic runners, aluminum foil, or boards on the sofa. Dogs don't like the feel of any of these things.

Digging

Dogs are natural diggers. They think of dirt as a sofa, a nesting bed, a cooling-off spa, a hunting ground, and an escape route. It helps if you can figure out exactly what motivates your particular Weim to dig; then you can find the answers. For example, if he's looking for a soft spot, he'll head for your garden. To manage the behaviour, you'll have to make the garden off-limits (fencing is a must) and supply a "digging box"—a sandbox made of soft earth for him to enjoy.

For overheated dogs, a baby pool is a welcome addition. But when it's really hot, bring the dog in the house during those 90°F (32°C) summer days. There are also "cooling blankets" that you might want to employ.

If your dog is trying to escape, he'll be digging near the fence line, so you may have to reinforce the fence by pouring 6 inches (15 cm) of concrete underneath it.

Many people divide their gardens into "people areas" and "dog areas" and separate them by a fence. This is a last resort, but it will work. If your dog makes a trail through your garden, don't try to replant over it—just turn it into a path.

Dog on the Sofa

It's no mystery why dogs enjoy the comfort of the living room sofa. It's high up and it's comfortable—especially on those cold winter days. When dogs were wolves, the alpha wolf always chose higher ground from which he could guard his pack and spot far-off game.

Unless you have a submissive dog or are sure of your own leadership, it's probably not a good idea to allow your dog to sleep on the sofa. In some cases, doing so can convince him that this place belongs to him by rights rather than sufferance, and some will stubbornly refuse to vacate, even with a firm warning. If the situation is badly managed, the dog may even growl or snap. To avoid this altogether, keep your dog on the floor or in his own bed.

Fearfulness

Because of genetic heritage or poor socialisation, some dogs are fearful. While you may never be able to turn a timid Weim into a completely confident animal, there are things that you can do to minimise his fearfulness. First, make sure that your Weim knows his basic obedience commands so that he will have something to focus on other than his fear. Then, start enhancing his social skills by introducing him to strangers—at a distance. Reward him for staying calm, and gradually have the person move in closer. You can also try it the other way—have the person stand still and ask your dog to approach. Keep the dog moving in a circular pattern, and use treats. Ask the stranger to drop a treat near him, and so on. Make sure that the stranger does not stare at your dog—in the canine world, staring is an aggressive act. Have her look off unconcernedly into the middle distance. Your Weim should gradually grow accustomed to meeting new people.

Inappropriate Toileting

Just because your dog is housetrained doesn't mean that your troubles are necessarily over in that department. About 20 percent of all problem behaviours in dogs fall into the category of "inappropriate toileting," a phrase that refers to the disconcerting habit of urination or defecation inside the home. (In some cases, this behaviour is simply "marking," a practice usually but not always restricted to intact males.) Most dogs relieve themselves outside, but when it occurs inside, it's a problem. It usually happens when there are strange dogs in the house or when something stressful has occurred at home. It can be corrected in exactly the same way that you would correct a puppy who makes a mistake.

Decide when he's a puppy if you are going to let your Weim on the sofa.

Accidents are to be expected in young puppies, of course, but when adult dogs engage in the same behaviour, you need to look further than the tiny bladder, weak sphincter muscles, and ignorance of a puppy.

If your previously housetrained dog reverts to this behaviour, you need to figure out what precipitated it. It is possible, for instance, that you simply have not been paying enough attention to his signals to go out, or perhaps he is left alone too long to "hold it." (Put yourself in his place. How

long would you like to be left without access to a bathroom?) Also, dogs who have insufficient "potty time" may be at a high risk of developing bladder stones. In any case, a dog who makes a mistake because he is left alone too long or who has given signals that you ignore does not have a problem. This is something that you need to handle by changing your schedule or by simply paying more attention.

House soiling also can have several medical causes, including bladder infections, bladder stones, diabetes, Cushing's disease, canine cognitive dysfunction in geriatric dogs, parasites, gastroenteritis, and problems with the pancreas. Even some medicines or a change in diet can cause it! If your dog suddenly begins relieving himself in the house, it's time for a vet checkup.

Male dogs also may engage in "marking behaviour," leaving a small amount of urine in strategic places around the house. This is most likely to occur when two or more males share a home. It's most common in unneutered males, but neutered dogs (and in a few cases, even females) may wish to "compete" in this game. It is more common when a new dog comes to stay or visit. To correct this habit, you should make sure that the dogs know that *you* are the leader of the house and that marking "their" territory is useless. Housetrain the dog as you would a new puppy, taking him *outside* when you catch him in the act and cleaning any marked areas very thoroughly with a nonammonia-based cleaner.

Some dogs urinate when they are very excited, but this behaviour is more typical of young puppies who just can't hold it. Just ignore the behaviour and the dog will soon outgrow it when his sphincter muscles get stronger.

Thunderphobia

Like other members of the sporting breeds, Weims may be very nervous about thunderstorms. They know that it's not safe to be out in them, and they aren't too convinced that your home provides adequate shelter either. Dogs who fear thunderstorms (or other loud noises) may seek your attention, hide behind the toilet, or try to run away.

Don't reassure your dog during a fearful event with petting, soothing words, or extra attention. That merely confirms his suspicion that something is really wrong. Redirect your Weim by being happy and focused on something else. With mild cases, you can turn on the radio or just let the dog hide. Many people have found that plug-in or spray "dog appeasing pheromones" are very helpful.

Desensitisation to thunderstorms is difficult—it's just too hard to replicate the sound and barometric pressure changes of thunderstorms. Your dog's veterinarian or veterinary behaviourist may recommend anti-anxiety medication.

Unneutered males sometimes engage in "marking" behaviour.

Jumping Up

You know the routine. You come home or a beloved guest arrives, and the next thing you know, your Weimaraner is making ecstatic leaps in the air, more often than not making unwelcome contact with a person's face and head. But don't blame your dog. Many dogs jump because their owners have inadvertently taught them that is what they want. (Unfortunately, Weims can jump much too well for their hapless owners.)

If your Weim never received encouragement for doing this as a puppy, he wouldn't be doing it now. However, it's never too late to make a change, though it does require an unwavering consistency on the part of you and your guests to make it work. The best way to get your dog to stop jumping is not to reward that behaviour—not with a look, not with a sound, and certainly not a kick or knee in the chest! When your dog jumps, fold your arms and look away. Do not respond. If he continues, just walk away. Don't look at him. Ignore him. When he ceases to jump, immediately get down to his level and reward him with praise and attention. After a week or so, he will get the idea. The key is to make sure that everyone understands that this is the correct response. Only then will it work.

Puppy Nipping and Play Biting

While some puppy biting is teething behaviour, in most cases, it's a form of social play. (Teething behaviour is much more likely to be chewing than nipping.)

Does He Have SA?

If your dog engages in inappropriate toileting only when you are not home, you may have a dog with separation anxiety.

The key is what dog trainers call bite inhibition. Most puppies learn it in the litter from their littermates—one reason why taking home a puppy too early can lead to problems. Puppies learn valuable social skills from their littermates! Your job as owner is to give your dog plenty of opportunities for playing that do not involve nipping. Examples include fetch and retrieving games, swimming, and learning tricks. You even can buy chicken-flavoured soap bubbles that your dog can chase. On the other hand, wrestling and tug-of-war may encourage some dogs to bite or grab. (This depends on the dog.)

If your Weim tends to grab or play bite, it's up to you to teach him that dog teeth don't belong on human hands. (Well-socialised, bite-inhibited dogs, on the other hand, enjoy gently taking their owners' hands in their mouths and leading them around.) To help your dog understand this lesson, send out a pained "yelp" when he tries to nip you. If possible do not pull your hand away—this will encourage him to bite down harder, and he will think it's a game. Instead, you want him to remove his mouth. Most of the time, a sharp yelp lets a puppy know that he has made a mistake. However, you need to be consistent about this—it doesn't work to let your puppy play bite sometimes and not others. Don't use punishment to stop this behaviour—chances are that it will only increase aggression. Remember that your puppy is trying to play with you—he just doesn't know how yet.

If he gets overexcited and starts to play bite, you can try a short (30 seconds to 2 minutes) "time-out." Leave the room—without your dog. He'll quickly figure out that nipping results in the end of play and learn to inhibit his bite.

Separation Anxiety

Canine separation anxiety (SA) is a behavioural disorder characterised by a dog who panics or becomes terribly upset and nervous when left alone. Such dogs are pathologically attached to their owners. SA dogs are destructive and may attempt to flee the home—some dogs have been known to go through windows! This behaviour is a mark of a dog's fear—not some attempt to "get back" or take revenge upon his owners, although it may seem like that. Weimaraners are extremely prone to this disorder because they were bred to be deeply dependent upon humans for their well-being and happiness.

Dogs who typically exhibit separation anxiety share several of these characteristics:

- acquired by the owner after three months of age or before six weeks of age
- orphaned or hand-raised
- acquired from a rescue centre, and/or has had several different homes/owners

Dogs with separation anxiety are often "Velcro" dogs while their owners are home because they follow them about everywhere. They become anxious at signs that their owners are leaving, and they begin to whine and cry almost immediately (and without ceasing) when their owners do go. They may yip in a high-pitched tone, defecate or urinate in the home, destroy property, and refuse to eat in their owners' absence. (These behaviours begin within 30 minutes after an owner leaves. If your dog displays these behaviours while you are home, he probably does not have separation anxiety. In addition, a dog with separation anxiety becomes overenthusiastic upon your return.)

To desensitise your dog to your departure, you need to rehearse it.

If you don't want your adult Weim to jump on people, you must discourage him as a puppy.

1. First, imitate your daily departure routine, including all the prep work. Then leave.
2. Give your dog a very special, high-value treat that he gets only while you are absent from the home—something stuffed with good cheese or even meat.
3. Don't make a big, anxiety-filled ordeal about leaving. Just say "Good-bye, Fido," and take off. Come back in 15 seconds—before he knows what hit him. Praise him if he has been quiet and nondestructive.
4. Then leave again. Continue until your dog stops barking. Over a period of weeks, you leave for longer and longer times.

Don't try to do this too fast—expect it to take a long time. In

Dogs with separation anxiety often become anxious at signs their owners are leaving.

addition, never punish a dog for having separation anxiety. That will only make it worse. You also can encourage independent play in your Weim by providing him with interesting toys that do not require human interaction.

Self-Mutilation

Self-mutilation such as acral lick dermatitis occurs when dogs lick or bite themselves excessively. You will see hair loss, sores, or rashes on the affected part of the body. The causes may be medical or psychological. If the former, the condition will usually resolve once the underlying condition is treated, although the behaviour may stay on even after the medical problem is addressed. For instance, acral lick dermatitis may begin as a simple fleabite or infection but progress to an obsession in which the dog cannot leave his foot alone. This is considered an obsessive-compulsive disorder.

Other factors that may lead to self-mutilation are anxiety, stress caused by long periods of confinement, isolation, harassment from another pet, or repeated exposure to scary noises. Your vet will do a physical exam and perhaps take a skin scraping or test for allergies. She may ask for a blood test or chemistry profile. If medical causes are ruled out, she will recommend that you do your best to remove the stressors in your dog's life. In some cases, anti-obsessional medication like serotonin reuptake inhibitors may be recommended. They help a lot.

7

ADVANCED TRAINING
AND ACTIVITIES
With Your Weimaraner

Your Weimaraner is just too great to keep yourself or to have lounging around the house all day. Once the two of you have mastered the basic skills of civilisation, it may be time to try some more adventurous sports. Whether your game is flyball, flying disc, or field trials, you'll both have a great time. However, before you jump into a new activity, there are a few things you need to keep in mind:

- Research the activity. Figure out if you have the time, money, energy, or even a real interest in whatever activity you're considering.
- Make sure that your Weim undergoes a thorough veterinary checkup.
- Start slowly. Even if your Weim gets a clean bill of health, go slowly, just as a human athlete would. Don't stress your dog beyond his natural limits.
- If your dog will be doing endurance work, beef up his fat and protein intake.
- Quit when you've had enough. Remember, you are both supposed to be having fun!

AGILITY

Agility is one of the fastest growing sports for dogs, and one of the most exciting, fast-paced canine sports for spectators. It is an extension of obedience but without all the formality and precision. Agility courses are more reminiscent of equestrian courses that include assorted jumps and hurdles. In agility, dogs demonstrate their agile nature and versatility by manoeuvring through a timed obstacle course of jumps, tunnels, A-frames, weave poles, see-saws, ramps, and a pause box. Unlike the higher levels of obedience, agility handlers are permitted to talk to their dogs, and even to give multiple commands.

There are a number of different levels of agility competition. Dogs progress from starters

Agility is a fast-paced sport where your dogs runs a timed obstacle course.

level, to novice, intermediate and advanced level. At each level, the courses are tougher, with increasingly difficult handling points.

The challenge of agility is to be able to control your dog in a wide-open area, and direct him to go where you want. It looks easy enough, but courses are set with twists, turns and sometimes with deliberate traps, which can tempt your dog to take the wrong course. If a dog takes the wrong course he is eliminated. He loses points for refusals, knocked poles, and missed contact points. The winner is the dog who completes a clear round in the fastest time.

Agility events in the UK are run under Kennel Club rules, and dogs are not allowed to compete until they are eighteen months old. This is a safeguard to protect bones and joints, which are vulnerable while a dog is still growing.

Even if you do not want to reach competitive level, you and your Yorkie can still enjoy agility as a fun, non-competitive pastime. Most training organisations have classes for beginners. You will need good basic obedience such as a solid "down", "wait" and "come" before you are ready to even start thinking about taking up agility at a fun level.

The number one consideration in an agility class is safety. This is one of the few sports that can result in serious injuries. Falling off an A-frame or dog walk can break bones. Neglecting to warm up before jumping can cause serious muscle injuries. Out-of-control dogs that are off-lead can also hurt other dogs.

Before you sign up for a class, visit one in action. Does the trainer emphasise safety? Are the larger dogs under control? If the answers are "yes" sign up! You and your Weimaraner will have a great time together.

If you want to start in agility with your dog your first port of call should be a local agility club, ring the secretary or instructor there and discuss your dog, the level of training you currently have and any health or fitness problems that your dog may suffer–agility is a physically demanding spot even at a fun level. Ask if you can come to watch the training and talk to people with experience, you may be invited to take your dog down so that he can be assessed for fitness and obedience. To find a local agility club in your area, contact the Kennel Club www.thekennelclub.org.uk or your local breed club. If you know other dog owners who take part in agility, word of mouth recommendation is also a great place to start, although you should always check the trainer or club's credentials yourself.

CANINE GOOD CITIZEN SCHEME

The Kennel Club's Good Citizen Dog Scheme is designed to promote and reward well-behaved dogs as community members. There are four levels to aim for: puppy foundation, bronze, silver and gold. The tests focus on basic good manners and include the following:

1. Accepting a friendly stranger: The friendly stranger will approach and greet the dog's handler. The dog must remain quiet.
2. Sitting politely for petting: This will occur while a friendly stranger pets the dog's head and body.
3. Appearance and grooming: This involves two steps. First, the evaluator checks that the dog is clean, groomed and in good condition. Then the dog must permit a stranger to comb or brush him and check his ears and front feet.
4. Out for a walk: This requires the dog to walk quietly on a loose lead, making several turns and stops.

The Canine Good Citizen test shows off your dog's good manners.

5. Walking through a crowd: This step requires the dog and handler to walk politely around and among at least three people.

6. Sit and down on command and staying in place: The dog is required to sit, lie down and stay on command.

7. Coming when called: This step requires the dog to stay on command and then come when called from a set distance.

8. Reaction to another dog: The dog should react with only casual interest when meeting another dog and handler.

9. Reaction to distraction: The dog should react calmly to two

common distractions (for instance, a chair falling over, a jogger running by, a wheeled cart passing by, or a dropped crutch or walking stick).

10. Supervised separation: The dog should remain calm when left with the evaluator while his handler goes out of sight for three minutes.

Field trials test your Weim's ability to point and retrieve birds.

During the tests, the dog must wear a properly fitted collar made of leather, fabric, or chain, and he will be on lead for most of the exercises the dog must also have an up-to-date ID tag with your name and contact details. Remember to bring your dog's brush or comb for the grooming section.

Don't give up if your dog doesn't pass the test on the first attempt—you'll know what you need to work on in the future! Keep training, have fun and try again later.

WORKING TRIALS

Working trials are an excellent opportunity to stimulate your Weimaraner's mental and physical natural abilities. Working trials is a competitive discipline in which dogs are assessed on a variety of working skills and abilities. Dogs must progress through levels of increasing difficulty known as "stakes". The stakes are; Companion Dog (CD), Utility Dog (UD), Working Dog (WD), Tracking Dog (TD), and Patrol Dog (PD).

Each stake is comprised of three sections: nosework, agility and control. Nosework tests the dog's ability to follow a scent trail.

Agility, as the name suggests, assesses a dog's physical agility. Canine competitors have to successfully negotiate a number of obstacles, including jumps and a scale.

The control section involves some traditional obedience-style exercises, including heelwork, a sendaway and a retrieve.

In the Patrol Dog stake, there is an extra section called manwork, in which the dog must successfully apprehend and control a 'criminal'.

Points are awarded for each exercise, and if the dog is awarded enough points, he achieves the title for that stake and is eligible for entry into the next level. The dog must obtain a minimum of 70 percent of the marks available in each section, as well as 80 percent or more of the total marks overall, to be awarded the Excellent qualification in each stake e.g. CDex, UDex, etc. Except for the CD the dog must first gain a Certificate of Merit at an Open Trial to enable him to compete in the relevant Championship Stake.

In the US, there are no working trials. Instead, agility and obedience form competitive sports in their own right and there is an extra discipline of tracking tests. To earn the title Tracking Dog (TD), the dog must pass a tracking test that involves following a scent trail of between 400 and 450 metres (440 and 500 yards) that was laid between thirty minutes and two hours earlier. He can then proceed to the Tracking Dog Excellent tracking test to earn the title Tracking Dog Excellent (TDX). At this level, the track will be longer, include more changes of direction, and will have been laid for a longer period before the dog is allowed to start following. The next level is the Variable Surface Tracking test, which shows that a dog has demonstrated his ability to follow a scent on a variety of different surfaces, including an urban setting. A Champion Tracker (CT) is a dog who has earned all three tracking titles.

Unlike obedience and agility titles that require a dog and handler to qualify three times, a Weimaraner only needs to complete one track successfully to earn each title.

GUNDOG WORKING TESTS

Gundog Working Tests are designed to test a dog's natural working ability while promoting sound gundog work. There are three different types of Gundog Working Tests, and each is designed for diferent breeds of dog.

FLYBALL

Flyball is a relay race with four-dog teams. A green light goes on at the starting line, and each dog races up a 51-foot (15 m) lane with four sets of hurdles ranging in height from 8 to 16 inches (20 to 41 cm). The hurdle height is based on the shortest dog on the team. At the end of the lane, a machine launches a tennis ball that the dog has to catch in mid-air and then return to the starting point, clearing all hurdles. Then, the next dog begins. The winning team completes the course the fastest. All breeds, including Weimaraners, are eligible to compete, but the best breeds are usually short, fast dogs like Parson Russell Terriers.

FLYING DISC

Many people lie to throw flying discs for their dogs to chase and catch, but for some people, disc sports are more than a back garden pastime. Their enthusiasm and athleticism of make them naturals in this sport.

Retrieving dumbbells is one part of obedience trials.

In the UK, there are some demonstrations of disc catching, but it is not recognised as a sport in its own right. Canine disc events throughout the world are sanctioned by the International Disc Dog Handlers' Association (IDDHA). Before you can compete for titles, you and your dog must demonstrate basic teamwork by successfully completing a test programme. You may then compete for titles, including the BDD (Basic Disc Dog), CSF (Combined Skills Freestyle title), and DDX (Disc Dog Expert).

FREESTYLE

Have you ever wanted to dance with your dog? Now you can dance the night away and compete for titles and prizes to boot. The relatively new sport of canine musical freestyle combines obedience and dance to demonstrate teamwork and rapport between dog and handler. The handlers and many of the dogs wear costumes as they perform carefully choreographed routines set to music. Both handler and dog are judged on several parameters. These include:

- Content of routine
- Accuracy
- Overall impression

There are different types of routine that are judged in different classes. Heelwork to Music, as the name suggests, must contain a percentage of close work, with the dog working in a variety of positions, such as left of the handler, right, in front, behind, and to the side. Freestyle routines are more flamboyant, as the dog can work at any distance from the handler, and they often include spectacular moves.

In the UK, the sport is recognised by the Kennel Club and competitions are held throughout the year. Competitors begin in

starters and work their way up through novice and intermediate to advanced level. There is a competition held annually at Crufts that draws big crowds. If you want to find out more about dancing with dogs, go the Kennel Club website–www.thekennelclub.org.uk or go a specialised site such as www.caninefreestyle.co.uk.

Children and Showing

If you have children interested in working with your Weim, they can compete in events designed to display their dog-handling skills in Junior Showmanship classes.

FORMAL OBEDIENCE

The objective of dog obedience is to demonstrate teamwork between handler and dog. In the UK, competitive obedience is dominated by Border Collies and working sheepdogs, with some German Shepherd Dogs, Golden Retrievers and Labrador Retrievers. However, there is no reason that your Beagle shouldn't take part.

There are various levels of obedience in the UK, with each covering a range of abilities. These are pre-beginners, beginners, novice, Class A, Class B and Class C. Each level becomes progressively more demanding. There will be a winner in each level of class.

The Pre-beginners Class is for the least experienced in the obedience world. Competitors must perform five different obedience exercises, totalling 75 points. Points are deducted for faults within each exercise. The exercises include walking to heel, both on and off lead, recall, sit-stay, and down-stay.

The Beginners Class is for those who have succeeded at pre-beginners. This class includes all the exercises from the pre-beginners class but also includes retrieving an article. This takes the potential points total to 100 points.

The Novice Class contains all the elements from the Beginners class, and also includes a temperament test, in which the judge will run his hands over the dog. The points total for this class is also 100 points.

The Westminster Dog Show

Next to the Kentucky Derby, the Westminster Dog show is the oldest continuous sporting event held in the United States. The original "Westminster" was actually a bar in a hotel of the same name. (The hotel no longer exists.) The first members of the club were men who owned gun dogs, and even today, the logo of the show is a representation of Sensation, a pointer owned by one of the members, who had a legendary ability to point birds. In 1877, the club held its first dog show, called the "First Annual New York Bench Show of Dogs." Since 1883, the show has been held in Madison Square Garden. So far, a Weimaraner has not attained the title "Best in Show." But there's always next year!

Class A is similar to the Novice class, although the sit-stay and the down-stay exercises are longer and less encouragement and help is allowed form the handler. There is also a scent discrimination test, in which six cloths are laid down. The dog has to select the single cloth that has been marked with the handler's scent. There is a total of 150 points on offer in this class.

Class B is more involved than Class A. The off-lead heelwork performed in this class must include changes of pace. There is an additional exercise known as the sendaway, drop and recall. In this exercise the handler must send the dog away in one direction, order him to drop to the floor, then call him back. As in Class A, there are also exercises for the retrieve, scent discrimination, sit-stay and down-stay. There is also a stand-stay. The inclusion of additional exercises takes the points total to 200.

Class C is the master class of obedience competition, and offers a total of 300 points. It contains many of the elements of Class B but with many of the exercises being longer in the duration and with the judges allowing less room for error. One of the hardest exercises in Class C is distance control, in which the handler must get the dog to perform six different exercises while dog and handler are at least ten paces apart.

There are three different types of obedience tests or shows. These are limited obedience shows, open obedience shows, and championship obedience shows. Competition becomes successively more difficult through these tests. There may be different classes scheduled at each show, from Pre-beginners through to Class C.

Go Solo at First

It's fun to go to a show just to look around. Don't bring your own dog to the show, however, unless he is entered. Most shows have a rule against this practice because space is limited.

Dog shows judge how closely a dog conforms to the breed standard.

RALLY OBEDIENCE

On January 1st 2005, rally became a titled event in the American Kennel Club. Rally is a sport held in conjunction with obedience in which a dog and handler proceed at their own pace through a course of directional signs in a manner similar to rally car racing. These signs are numbered sequentially to show the handler where to take the dog. The dog and handler team heel from sign to sign and perform the exercises indicated on the

If you and your dog are still learning, it's fun to enter a "match" rather than a show. Matches are informal affairs, and you can enter the very day of the event. They are specifically designed for inept handlers and novice dogs, which makes them a great way to learn the ropes. You won't receive any "points" for winning, however, even if your dog turns out to be Best in Match.

sign at each location. Each sign contains an exercise illustrated with symbols.

Your dog can earn a title in each of three levels: Novice, Advanced and Excellent. This sport is just taking off in the United States; if it proves popular it could well find its way to the United Kingdom.

SHOWING (CONFORMATION)

When dog fanciers use the phrase "dog show", they are usually referring to conformation shows, which are basically beauty contests. The avowed purpose of the conformation show is to identify those dogs that most closely resemble the breed standard–a written description of the "perfect" dog–and those who are worthy to pass along their genes to the next generation.

Dog shows pop up all around the country every weekend, and they provide a great opportunity to meet people, exhibit your dog, buy great dog stuff you can't get anywhere else, and learn a lot about dogs in general. Most people handle their own dogs, while others hire a professional. However, if you are planning to handle your dog yourself, consider taking some ringcraft classes at your local training club and attend a few dog shows. Ringcraft classes can be invaluable. You'll learn dog show protocol, dress, and terminology, and you'll learn how to gait and pose your dog.

Even children can compete in events designed to display their dog-handling skills in Junior Handling Classes.

The first great objective of showing dogs is to make your dog up into a champion. Each breed competes separately towards that goal.

In the United Kingdom, a dog must win three Challenge Certificates (CCs) from three different judges, with one of these Certificates being awarded after the age of one year. To win a CC, a dog must already have been chosen for Best of Sex.

Although it sounds simple, earning the CC in the United Kingdom is not easy, because not all shows offer these certificates. CCs are allocated by the Kennel Club based on the popularity of the breeds being shown. Additionally, dogs that have already earned a CC can continue to compete for more certificates. It is not uncommon in KC shows for dogs that win frequently at the breed, group, and best-in-show level to never become Champions.

To earn an AKC Champion title, a dog must beat other dogs in multiple age and gender classes to become Winners Dog or

Winners Bitch. Based on how many dogs are beaten, points, up to a maximum of five at one time, are earned. Some of the points won must be "majors", in which the dog earns three or more points in a single-breed class. A total of fifteen points, with two majors, are necessary to become a Champion of Record.

While dogs don't have to do tricks to win at a conformation show, they need to show basic good manners. Your dog will need to become accustomed to having a stranger check him out, including teeth, and in the cases of males, testicles. Make sure your friendly Weimaraner leaves other dogs strictly alone–there is no sniffing and socialising allowed. It is just possible an untoward disagreement might occur.

Trail Biking Is Best

Weims do best as trail riding, rather than street biking, companions—their paws are not meant for running over pavement, and the traffic is too dangerous.

THERAPY DOGS

Therapy dogs visit people in nursing homes, hospitals, and rehabilitation centres to brighten spirits. (therapy work does wonders for the dogs' spirits too.) Petting a dog reduces blood pressure and physical stress, so it helps ill patients to heal.

Calm Beagles make lovely therapy dogs. They are so intuitively tuned in to people that they know when someone is not feeling well physically, or when they're feeling low. They are also small enough that they can cuddle in beds, sit on laps in wheelchairs, and help children who are afraid of big dogs. Older dogs who may not be physically fit enough for sports competitions may find that therapy is just the ticket.

Therapy dogs can make a significant difference to someone's life during an illness or hospital stay. Residents of rest homes that have live-in therapy dogs or who are visited by therapy dogs tend to be happier and healthier. Being able to pet a dog takes people's thoughts away from themselves for a while, and it helps lower the high blood pressure related to the stress of being ill or ageing.

Children's hospitals that use therapy dog visits usually mention the programme at admission. Having a dog nuzzle up to a child

With a few safety precautions, your Weim can be the perfect camping partner.

who is bald or has a lot of attached tubes helps that child attain some sense of normality, a sense that every minute of every day is not about being sick. Often, particularly for children, seeing dogs removes a lot of worry about what they look like while they're sick.

Many children and adults miss their dogs at home, and therapy dogs give them an opportunity to tell the handler about the dogs they miss. Just petting a dog makes people feel calmer; calmer people experience less stress than worried people and they heal faster. Think about what your reaction would be if you were sick and someone brought in their Beagle to see you: wouldn't you forget your woes for a bit while petting such a gorgeous coat and looking at that lovely face?

Therapy dogs also visit rest homes or hospice centres where people don't expect to ever leave. In these situations, dogs bring a sense of joy and a fond remembrance of life to a dull routine that can have frightening moments. Dogs are vibrant and totally in the present moment. They don't worry about this afternoon, much less tomorrow. Dogs help people feel more in the moment too. For the facing interminable days in the hospital, or knowing they're never going to improve, these moments have great meaning and value.

In the UK, the governing body for therapy dogs is Pets as

The Weim's stamina and natural athleticism make him a great jogging partner.

Therapy (PAT). For detailed information on registering your dog as a PAT dog, visit their website (www.petsastherapy.org). A dog must be a minimum of nine months of age before applying to be a therapy dog. A registered evaluator will check on the dog's general health and temperament. The dog will then be tested to see if he will walk on a loose lead, remain under control despite distractions, and not react to loud or sudden noises. The evaluator will also check to see if the dog is happy to be groomed, as this shows whether dog will accept all over handling and touching. Once your dog is accepted to work as a PAT dog, you can approach local hospitals and care homes and make arrangements to start visiting.

Weim Scootering

Scootering is one of the newest and best ways to enjoy exercising your Weimaraner. You need nothing fancier than a scooter and an x-back sled harness. You ride, he runs and pulls, and you have the Iditarod without the cold and snow. Perfect. Mush on!

THE SIMPLER PLEASURES

Of course, you needn't get involved in "official" events to get out and have some fun with your Weimaraner.

Fun at the Park

If you live in an urban area or don't have a way to get your Weim out into the country, you can't do better than a regular visit to your local park. Here is a place where your Weimaraner can run around to meet other dogs as well as work off some of that boundless energy (and perhaps poundage, too). However, do not take your Weim out to meet other dogs unless you know that he enjoys their company. While neutral ground like a park is not usually a place where dogs fight, it can and does happen.

Good sense and good manners (and they are remarkably the same) dictate that visitors to parks observe a few simple rules to make their stay more productive and stress free. The first rule is that of "omission." Don't bring very young dogs, unvaccinated dogs, sick dogs, or females in heat. Take no more dogs than you can reasonably handle.

This is the time to take the lead off your Weim! Let him run about exploring his new world. Go with him, of course. There's no point in taking your dog to a park if he just has to stay on the lead. In addition, many dogs feel threatened by other dogs when they are on lead. Their normal "flight-or-fight" instinct is interrupted, and the dominant Weim may become aggressive as he is being investigated by other, off-lead dogs.

Biking

A Weimaraner makes one of the best trail-biking partners. A well-conditioned Weim in his prime (between the ages of two and five) moves at about 10 miles (16 km) an hour for an hour or more. Keep a careful eye on him—if he starts to lag or slow down, you know it's time to take a break.

Make frequent stops for water breaks, and keep your eye out for dangerous wildlife and aggressive dogs who may attack anything running. Probably the most common canine injury in biking, however, is worn-down pads. Your can buy a spray product like Pad Guard that you can apply directly to your dog's feet that forms a protective barrier. I think it works better than booties for this purpose.

Camping

Nothing beats sleeping under the stars with your faithful best friend snoozing at your side. Don't count on your Weim to protect you, however.

One of the hardest things for dogs to accept-especially in populated areas like parks-is relaxed isolation.

Moreover, if your dog is in your tent with you, you can keep each other warm. When you leave your cosy campsite, clean up; be sure to check around for dog waste and remove it. If you found the campsite lovely, others will too. Don't ruin it for them.

Of course, it's important to check ahead to make sure that the campground allows dogs, and under what conditions. Most require dogs to be kept leaded, but policies can change from year to year. Carry a recent picture of your dog. It's not enough to say that you've lost your Weimaraner. Believe it or not, many people don't know a Weimaraner from a wombat.

Pack for the weather—and expect the unexpected. Thunderstorms, high winds, and blizzards can come seemingly out of nowhere. A jacket for your Weim will be appreciated in cold weather.

A campfire can be fatally attractive to dogs—especially if they are redolent with the smell of cooking sausages. Ashes remain hot for hours, so monitor your dog at all times. If he will be swimming, check out the currents and provide your dog with a flotation device. And be considerate of others—don't allow your dog to bark or wander.

Your camping partner should be up to date on vaccinations, including Lyme disease if you are entering a tick-infested area—which is practically anywhere in the woods. And of course he should carry plenty of identification. Bring insect repellent and be sure that your dog is on a tick and flea programme.

Because you'll be bringing a first-aid kit for yourself, include antibiotic ointment, Vetrap (an elastic bandage that sticks only to itself and can hold bandages in places without pins or adhesive tapes), and Benadryl for bee stings.

Carry adequate food and water for your dog, and pack everything up in a fox-proof container.

Hiking

Nothing is more primal than a brisk and adventurous hike with your Weim. (Puppies less than five months of age should be taken on short hikes only, though.) If the day is cool and you have plenty of water for both of you, you are all set. Temperatures above 80°F (26°C) are probably too warm for a tough hike. Keep your dog on a lead for his protection.

Avoiding Tent Trouble

If you have never camped with your dog before, set up the tent in your backyard and let your dog check it out. Besides, you can use the practice yourself.

A face like this can bring comfort and joy to those who may no longer be able to care for an animal.

Jogging

Weimaraners are perfect running and jogging partners, and although they have tremendous speed and endurance, they are not machines. They need proper conditioning, and when exercising, lots of fluids to keep them fit. Left to their own devices, they'll drink water from any dirty puddle or contaminated waterway, so you need to make sure that your dog is well hydrated with healthy fluids. You can give your jogging partner water or even a special sports drink formulated for dogs called Rebound. While some people carry along a portable dish and water, you also can teach your pooch to drink from a water bottle, just as you do!

To train your dog to do this, start when he is pretty thirsty already; otherwise, he'll be convinced that you are tormenting him. To familiarize him with the process, let him watch you squirt some of the water into his familiar but empty dog bowl, and let him drink. Keep the bottle low at this point so that his head is down in the normal drinking position. Squirt the water slowly so that he doesn't become nervous. He'll still want more because you squirted just a bit into the bowl. Now, squirt it again while he is drinking. Do this slowly enough so that he becomes impatient with the process and soon begins to lick from the bottle. When he does, turn the bottle sideways. (You don't want to pour the water down his throat.) You can gradually raise the bottle a bit higher but not more than parallel to the ground.

8

HEALTH

of Your Weimaraner

Health and happiness go hand in hand. The more you know about dog wellness, the better you will be able to provide your Weim the kind of life he needs and deserves.

YOU AND YOUR VET

Your veterinarian is your partner in helping you to maintain your dog's health. Taking your dog to see the vet regularly is absolutely critical. Even if he is not scheduled for a vaccination, regular checkups are a must. This is basic preventive medicine. Young dogs need yearly exams, while dogs older than six should have wellness checkups twice yearly. Not only do dogs age faster than people—their diseases usually progress much faster as well. Moreover, many early signs of heart, liver, or kidney disease are subtle, and dogs often will attempt to hide them as a matter of instinctive self protection.

During the exam, your vet will check for abnormalities. She may move from the front to the rear of the dog, looking at the eyes, ears, nose, throat, lungs, heart, and GI tract and checking for lumps during the whole process. (Weimaraners are known for their predisposition to get lumps.) The vet also will do a faecal examination every year to check for worms, if requested.

Normal Values

On the first visit to the vet, she may check for normal canine values, although there are broad limits as to what constitutes normal; what is normal for your Weim might be abnormal for another dog. Your vet will be able to see from her records what a normal pulse, temperature, and blood count are for your particular dog. Some of the values that she might take include capillary refill time, mucous membrane and gum colour, rectal temperature, pulse rate, respiratory rate, and level of hydration.

Capillary Refill Time

Capillary refill time (CRT) is the time that it takes for the capillaries to refill with blood. Capillary refill time is measured by pressing on the gums over the canine tooth with one finger and seeing how long it takes for normal colour to return. Normal is about one second. A CRT that is longer than one second may indicate poor circulation, while longer than 3 seconds may be a sign of shock.

Mucous Membrane and Gum Colour

Healthy Weims usually have pink membranes. Pale, dark red, or yellowish colour may signal disease. To check this yourself, just lift your Weim's lip and observe the colour of the inner lip and gums.

Rectal Temperature

A rectal temperature of 101° to 102°F (38° to 39.1°C) is normal. Use a canine or paediatric rectal thermometer lubricated with petroleum jelly. Hold the thermometer in place for one to two minutes. Don't rely on the "cold nose" theory of dog wellness. A dog could have a cool nose and a burning fever. However, warm ears *could* be an indication of fever, just as very cold ears may indicate hypothermia. Hypothermia is indicated by a temperature below 99.5°F (37.5°C) and hyperthermia by a temperature above 102.4°F (39.1°C).

Your Weim should have yearly vet checkups throughout his life.

Pulse Rate (at Rest)

A young dog's pulse should be 110 to 120 beats per minute; an adult's pulse rate should be 60 to 80 beats per minute.

Respiratory Rate

For puppies, the rate should be 20 to 25 breaths per minute; adults should take 14 to 16 breaths per minute. Slow or fast gasping breathing may indicate a serious problem. If your dog's abdomen expands instead of the chest when he inhales, he is not breathing normally.

Hydration

To determine whether a dog is sufficiently hydrated, grasp the skin over the back, pull up and release. It should return to its position within one second.

Vaccines have saved the lives of millions of dogs.

VACCINES

Along with antibiotics and anaesthesia, vaccines are probably the greatest medical invention ever. They have saved countless lives of both humans and dogs. To take only one example, canine distemper is the greatest worldwide killer of dogs. Yet in this country, most young veterinarians have never seen a case, and the reason is that dogs are generally well vaccinated. The same cannot be said for dogs in other, less-developed parts of the world. Today, dogs are often vaccinated against the following diseases.

Adenovirus

Also called infectious hepatitis, this now rare disease (thanks to vaccines) causes abdominal pain, vomiting, liver damage, and eye inflammation. Your vet will vaccinate your dog against the disease in the initial puppy series of vaccinations.

Canine Parvovirus

The first parvovirus (CPV-1) strain appeared suddenly in the canine world in 1967 but affected only newborn puppies. A stronger, nastier version (CPV-2) showed up in 1978 and began to kill dogs

Pet Insurance

It is possible to buy pet insurance for your dog, although currently only about 3 percent of dog owners do so. Pet insurance policies work just about the same way human insurance works: Pet insurance companies charge premiums, and there are deductibles for different policy plans. Routine veterinary checkups may not be covered in the base plan, but they may be offered as an addition. There may be exclusions for older animals, pre-existing conditions, and breed-related problems. Basic policies generally cover treatment for accidents, injuries, and illnesses. Some cover acupuncture and chiropractic treatments. Some cover neutering. Some cover dental work. Read over any policy carefully and ask questions. Of course, make sure that your vet accepts pet insurance.

around the world. (Researchers think that it's a mutation from the feline distemper virus.)

"Parvovirus" means "small virus," but this disease can mean big trouble for your Weimaraner. It affects most members of the dog family, including foxes, and specialises in attacking rapidly dividing host cells, such as those found in the intestine, bone marrow, lymph system, and foetal cells. Unlike most other viruses, parvoviruses don't coat themselves in fat—and for complicated reasons, this makes them hard to destroy by conventional means. This tough virus is found absolutely everywhere in the environment. Parvo causes severe vomiting and bloody diarrhoea. Puppies can easily die from dehydration.

Distemper

Distemper is a highly contagious viral disease of worldwide distribution. While domestic dogs are the most frequent victims, other species, including ferrets, and even sea lions, also can be affected. It is spread mostly by direct contact from dog to dog, but coughing can spread the virus over short distances. The main signs of the disease include fever, loss of appetite, diarrhoea, vomiting, a thick yellow discharge from the nose and eyes, coughing, and seizures. A blood test can be performed for confirmation that a dog has distemper.

While there is no drug that can cure the disease (it's caused by a virus), a vet may prescribe antibiotics to fight off secondary bacterial infections. Intravenous fluids, cough suppressants, and drugs to control seizures also may be administered, usually within the confines of a veterinary hospital. Even dogs who survive the disease may not fully recover; some animals have persistent nervous twitches and seizures.

As always, the best cure is prevention. A very effective vaccine is given to puppies, beginning as young as five weeks, in a series of three to five injections. Revaccination is performed at one year and possibly again at two years and every three years thereafter.

Leptospirosis

Leptospirosis is spread when abraded skin comes in contact with dog urine. The spirochetes (*Leptospira interrogans*) travel up the bloodstream, causing fever, joint pain, and general sickness. The organism settles in the kidneys, and some kinds affect the liver, too. The disease is life threatening, and yes, you can catch it from your dog.

Luckily for humans, leptospirosis is not nearly as dangerous to people as it is to canines.

The tricky thing is that leptospirosis has been classified into subtypes called servovars, and there are more than 200 of them. Luckily, *Leptospira interrogans* responds to penicillin. Sometimes, a combination of a penicillin with a fluroquinolone-type antibiotic is used to clear both the bloodstream and the kidneys of the infection.

Vaccination against *Leptospira interrogans* is currently available for the canicola, grippotyphosa, pomona, and icterohaemorragiae serovars. They often are included in the basic "distemper," or DHLPP, shot. Vaccination will reduce the severity of disease but will not prevent infected dogs from becoming carriers. Unfortunately, some dogs are sensitive to this vaccine, and they develop hives or other serious allergic reactions such as anaphylactic shock. To make things worse, recent outbreaks involve serovars for which vaccines do not exist. Discuss with your veterinarian the advisability of this vaccine for your dog.

Vaccinate Wisely

A debate is currently ongoing as to what is the safest vaccination protocol. Talk to your vet about what you can do for your Weim, taking into consideration the advice in this book. Your vet can keep you on track with what's necessary for your Weim.

Kennel Cough

Kennel cough *(infectious tracheobronchitis)* is a highly contagious respiratory condition thought to be caused by the bordetella bacterium. Dogs with this highly annoying but not usually serious condition cough and sometimes produce a gunky mucus or phlegm discharge for two weeks or so. Other than that, the dog doesn't feel very ill and goes about his regular routine with little trouble. In a few cases, a secondary infection inducing pneumonia may occur. Your vet may prescribe antibiotics, but there's no cure for kennel cough itself except time, and you should try to get your dog to rest if he is diagnosed with it. Because it is so highly contagious, an infected dog should be strictly kept away from others. Some people give a cough suppressant to stop the coughing, but this is not always appropriate. The dog should cough out the nasty phlegm. However, follow your veterinarian's advice. Clean up with bleach.

While kennel cough vaccines may not be necessary for a dog who stays at

If you show your Weim, he should be vaccinated for kennel cough.

home and never meets other dogs, your Weim should be vaccinated if:

- You plan to board him. (It's a requirement of most boarding facilities.)
- He participates in canine activities like agility, conformation, or field trials.
- He takes group obedience classes.
- He goes to doggy daycare.

Two types of vaccines are available: injectable and intranasal. The intranasal works faster and is the best choice for most dogs. Dogs can be vaccinated for kennel cough as early as four weeks of age. This is one vaccine that should be given about every six months for best effect.

Rabies

Rabies is a deadly virus that is contagious to all mammals, including people. It is most frequently transmitted through bite wounds. It then travels through the nerves, spinal cord, and eventually the brain, a process that may take weeks to months. After reaching the brain, however, the virus causes death within ten days.

You'll probably never see rabies in a dog, as it is not present in the UK, but these are the signs:

- aberrant behaviour
- abnormal drooling
- aggression
- lethargy
- seizures

Once signs of rabies develop, there is no cure. The disease is fatal. If you are travelling overseas you will need to speak to your vet about vaccination.

Adverse Reactions to Vaccines

Like humans, animals can have an occasional bad reaction to a vaccine. In most cases, this is a minor allergic reaction resulting in hives and itching, although more severe reactions have been reported. Some experts have linked vaccinations to anaemia, platelet problems, and joint disease. It is believed that the number of pets who suffer the consequences is very low (between 1 in 1,000 and 1 in 10,000). However, it's hard to tell because there is no national database that allows veterinarians to report adverse vaccine reactions or to obtain information about adverse reactions to particular products.

In any event, it is safe to say that any side effects that some dogs experience from some vaccines are more than outweighed by the millions of lives that they save every year. Take rabies and distemper, for example, which used to be common killers. I bet you've never seen a dog with either one, and I hope you never will. Thank your veterinarian and his vaccination programme.

NEUTER!

To spay a female dog means to remove her reproductive organs. Castrated male dogs have their testicles removed. These procedures are safe and performed under anaesthesia, and your pet may be able to come home the same day. While a few people still contend that neutering is "unnatural" or even "cruel," this simple procedure will help your pet live a longer and healthier life. Spaying, for instance, eliminates the possibility of uterine or ovarian cancer and greatly reduces the incidence of breast cancer, especially when a pet is spayed before her first oestrous cycle. Castrating males eliminates the risk of testicular cancer and reduces the incidence of prostate disease. Neutered animals are much less likely to mark their territory, and they exhibit fewer problem behaviours (such as aggression) than do their intact counterparts. They also will be less likely to escape the confines of their homes. And don't worry—dogs don't seem to have any concept of "gender identity." They won't be traumatised.

Leishmaniasis: A Vaccine Is Coming!

Visceral leishmaniasis is fairly new to this country, but it is endemic around the Mediterranean, where it infects many dogs. The disease begins with a protozoan in the water. Signs include weight loss, enlargement of the liver and spleen, and arthritis. If a sand fly bites an infected dog and then attacks a person, that person can become very ill. Human beings also can contract the disease from sand flies, and in people, it is frequently lethal unless treatment is prompt. Recently, French scientists developed a vaccine that seems to lastingly protect dogs from the disease; it will help people as well.

Neutering is a simple procedure that can help your dog live a healthier life.

Not-So-Fun Flea Facts

The *Xenopsylla cheopis*, or rat flea, carries bubonic plague, and the *Pulex irritans*, or human flea, dines on swine. Both species will also chomp down on your dog.

Neutering also provides a valuable service to your community. Neutered animals will not produce litters of unwanted puppies to burden overcrowded shelters and breed rescues. If you choose to breed (and place the life of your female dog at risk for pyometra, mastitis, and other awful conditions), you are responsible for any puppies that result. If a buyer decides three or four years down the road that she no longer wants the dog, it's up to you to take him back. If you don't, you are part of the problem. Leave breeding to people who are working to improve Weimaraners as a breed.

PESTS AND INFECTIONS

A host of pests, both external and internal, can plague your Weim. Fortunately, there are lots of ways that you and your vet can work to keep your dog pest-free.

Fleas

Fleas (*ctenocephalides felis* and *ctenocephalides canis*) are fascinating and terrible creatures. They belong to the insect order *Siphonaptera*, which means "wingless siphon," a nice way of saying "bloodsucker." Worldwide, more than 2,000 species of fleas exist, and they have a four-stage life cycle: egg, larva, pupa, and adult. The species you'll commonly see on a dog is Ctenocephalides felis, cat flea. This is somewhat of a misnomer, because it really prefers dogs.

The flea spends its entire adult life on your dog. Fleas of both sexes eat blood, and they are able to fast for months. They are clever creatures, complete with tremendous jumping ability and high-tech antennae that can detect movement, heat, shadows, vibrations, and changes in air currents. All of this, of course, enables them to get their dinner. Flea eggs slide off the dog when he scratches and get deposited where they fall. These eggs develop wherever they have landed—into larva, pupa, and adult fleas. Under perfect conditions, the flea can complete its entire life cycle in two weeks.

Flea bites are irritating at best and can lead to severe itching and hair loss. A large infestation of them can cause serious anaemia in puppies, and to top it off, they can transmit all kinds of diseases, including plague, typhus, and tularaemia. They also carry parasites such as tapeworms. Some dogs are so hypersensitive to flea saliva that they will itch all over from the bite of a single flea. Flea dirt looks like specks of pepper on the dog's skin and is easily visible if you look carefully. If there is flea dirt, there are fleas.

Keeping Fleas Away

A healthy dog is flea-free, and prevention is the best way of accomplishing that. While adult fleas spend most of their horrible lives right on your dog, their eggs, larvae, and pupae can be found in cosy spots all over your home—rugs, upholstery, and bedding, not to mention the grass outside. And the pupae can lie dormant for months. It doesn't help that wild animals serve as a reservoir for fleas. Even when you successfully keep them off your dog, the fleas that live on your dogs also take up residence on rabbits and foxes.

All-Year Protection

Fleas aren't just summertime pests. Keep your dog on flea protection year round.

Luckily, you have a wide choice of flea killers that are safe for your dog. Some target adult fleas, while others are insect growth inhibitors. Some are safe for puppies.

If you find your house infested with fleas, must treat the whole environment. Vacuum your home thoroughly, especially in areas where your dog sleeps. Don't put a chopped-up flea collar in the vacuum or bedding as some people recommend—they can produce toxic fumes. (Throw out the vacuum bag right away.) If you know that you have a flea problem in the home, use a carpet powder or fogger to get rid of them. Don't forget to treat the car and pet carrier too! Wash the dog's bedding every week.

Check your dog for fleas and ticks after he's been outside.

If your garden harbours fleas, rake up organic debris like leaves and grass clippings. (Fleas like warm, moist shady places best.) If your dog likes to sleep under the porch, use a flea killer under there. It's best to use an environmentally gentle product, such as one with fenvalerate as its active ingredient.

To kill fleas on your dog, your best choice is usually a once-a-month topical applied to an area between the shoulder blades. Some kill fleas only, while others kill both ticks and fleas. Some of the most widely used and most natural flea killers are pyrethrins,

Follow the Directions

Once you choose your preferred flea-control product, use it properly—follow the directions on the label.

which are natural extracts made from chrysanthemums. Pyrethroids are synthetic pyrethrin compounds. They work longer than pyrethrins but not as quickly. (They also are dangerous to cats.) Imidacloprid and fipronil are newer insecticides used as a once-a-month topical medicine.

Other choices include sprays in an aerosol or pump bottle, powders, collars, dips, pills, and injectable products. Talk to your vet for the right flea-control approach for your Weimaraner.

Flies

Flies are more than just annoying and full of disease—they bite. Stable flies, blackflies, and deerflies are the most common culprits. They can cause a condition called "fly **strike**," which usually occurs in hunting **dogs and other animals that** spend a lot of time outside. It typically occurs as painful bites on the tips and top surface of the dog's ears, as well as on the bridge of the nose, where the skin is thinnest. (The flies are after your Weim's blood.) That's also a place where your dog has difficulty protecting himself. If you notice blood spots or flies around your dog's ears, assume that he is getting fly bites. In serious cases, the flies could lay **their eggs there and your dog** could get maggots!

If your dog has been attacked by flies, clean the area gently with warm water and a gentle antiseptic soap. Then apply a topical antibiotic. To prevent fly bites from happening in the first place, apply a topical insecticide safe for dogs to the area around the ears.

Hunting dogs can be prone to a condition called "fly strike."

Fungal Diseases

Blastomycosis

Blastomycosis is a systemic fungal disease of dogs, people, and other mammals. It can be mistaken for cancer, viral infections, and Lyme disease. Blasto is inhaled into a dog's lungs from digging in contaminated soil. It can cause weight loss, swollen lymph nodes, sores, coughing, lack of appetite, fever, and even blindness. If your dog exhibits signs of blasto, take him to the vet right away.

Ringworm

Ringworm is a fungus that can infect dogs, cats, and people. Several species exist, but most cases affecting dogs are caused by Microsporum canis, Microsporum gypseum, or Trichophyton mentagrophytes. The fungus is usually found either on the dog himself or in his living area. Spores from infected animals can be shed into the environment and live for more than 18 months. Ringworm is transmitted not only by direct contact with an infected animal; it also is transmitted with any item carrying the spores. The classic sign of ringworm is a small hairless lesion with scales in the centre. The lesion may grow in size. The best way to identify a ringworm infection is by collecting scales and crust from the skin and doing a culture. While isolated lesions will heal on their own within four months, more serious cases require treatment. Your veterinarian can advise you as to the best course of action. Ringworm is transmissible between dogs and people.

Intestinal Infections

Coccidia

Coccidia are microscopic, single-celled organisms that infect the intestine. They can cause watery and sometimes bloody diarrhoea, which can be dangerous in a puppy (because of fluid loss). They come from faecal-contaminated soil; the oocysts are swallowed when a dog licks dirt from himself. These later break open and release sporozoites that multiply in the intestinal cells. The infection is especially common where young animals are housed in close quarters.

If a sufficient number of coccidian are present, a routine faecal test will reveal infection. Small numbers may escape detection, and repeat tests need to be performed. Oddly enough, there is no medication that actually kills the coccidia; only the power of the immune system can do it. That is why the disease is most serious in puppies, who have an immature immune system. Older dogs seem able to control the disease. However, certain drugs called "coccidiostats" inhibit coccidial reproduction, which makes it easier for the immune system to work. This course of treatment takes some time to complete and could last for up to a month.

Single-Cell Specialists

As a rule, dogs and cats get infected with Isospora species of coccidian, while livestock get the Eimeria species. These species of coccidia do not cross over.

Coccidia is more dangerous in puppies than adults.

Cryptosporidium

Cryptosporidium is a lot like coccidia. In fact, until recently, they were believed to be simply another species of coccidia, but they are much worse. For one thing, the oocysts are so tiny that they are very hard to find under a microscope and often escape detection. However, a test kit has been developed that can detect all species of cryptosporidium.

The original oocysts are passed in the faeces of an infected animal, but once they are embedded in the animal, they can keep infecting the dog over and over again.

Treatment for this disease is difficult. Because they are not really coccidia, drugs that work on coccidia have no effect on cryptosporidium. They also resist bleach and most other cleansers. Only prolonged exposure to ammonia or extreme temperatures can kill them.

The good news is that cryptosporidium from dogs and cats seldom infect people. Humans have their own brand.

Mange

Mange is a disease caused by mites (which are arachnids related to spiders) that live inside hair follicles, a difficult area to medicate.

One kind of mange mite is called demodex, which is naturally found on the skin of practically all dogs. (They pick them up from their mothers during the first few days of life. Orphaned puppies raised by hand never get them.) However, they can sometimes overrun a dog who has an inherited immune defect or a dog who is on a medication that suppresses the immune system (like steroids). These dogs have a hard time fighting off the infection. Demodex used to be extremely costly and difficult to treat, but new medications are available that can often keep it under control. This mite is not contagious to people or to other adult dogs. Recent studies indicate that Weimaraners are among the ten most likely breeds to develop this condition.

However, another type of mite, sarcoptes (also known as scabies), is contagious to both people and dogs. This mite is easier to kill than is demodex, even though its symptoms (yellow, crusty skin and itching) are quite unpleasant.

Still another contagious mite is cheyletiella, which has signs similar to scabies. People can acquire it as well, but no treatment is usually needed because the mites die almost immediately. There's only a brief bout of itching.

Ticks

Ticks are arachnids, which means that they are more closely related to mites and spiders than they are to fleas, which are insects. All ticks have three pairs of legs as nymphs, but as adults they acquire another pair, to make eight legs altogether. They can't fly, but they possess a special organ called "Haller's organ" that detects odour, heat, and humidity—in other words, a potential victim. To attack their prey, they just climb on tall grass and wait.

About 850 species of tick exist worldwide, including the Lone Star tick (*Amblyomma americanum*), Gulf Coast tick (*Amblyomma maculatum*), moose tick (*Dermacentor albipictus*) Rocky Mountain spotted fever tick (*Dermacentor andersoni*), American dog tick (*Dermacentor variabilis*), brown dog tick (*Rhipicephalus sanguineus*), and the deer or black-legged tick (*Xodes scapularis*), which famously carries Lyme disease. Other species cause other serious diseases, including babesiosis (*piroplasmosis*), cytauxzoonosis, ehrlichiosis, haemobartonellosis, hepatozoonosis, Rocky Mountain spotted fever, tick paralysis and tularaemia.

If, despite your best efforts, you see a tick on your dog, remove it right away. Use tweezers or a special tick-removal instrument that will grab the tick without squeezing it and re-injecting its disgusting fluids back into your dog. Don't touch the tick with your bare hands. Grasp the tick with the tweezers as close to its head as you can and pull it straight out. Clean the wound with disinfectant and wash your hands. Throw the tick in the toilet and flush. You may notice redness and swelling at the site of the bite after you remove the tick. This comes from the irritating saliva, but it does not mean that the tick's head is embedded in the wound. That very seldom happens, actually. It should soon heal up.

To de-tick your dog's environment, treat both the garden and kennel area with an environmentally safe product containing fenvalerate every month during tick season. Don't spray where the run-off could get into a nearby stream, however. Remove leaves,

Don't Play Doctor

Never assume that a dog flea and tick product will work on your cat. You can seriously harm your cat by using a product containing permethrins, for instance. Also, do not combine different products unless the label or your vet tells you that it's okay to do so. They may cancel each other out or harm your dog. Even if you think you've gotten the flea problems beat, continue to use preventions. These pests can come back fast.

You can de-tick your garden with an environmentally safe lawn treatment.

brush, and tall grass in the area.

If your Weimaraner is exposed to the great outdoors, especially the woods, he will be exposed to ticks. Many antiflea products also kill ticks; check the label. Some products kill some species of tick but not others. In severely infested area, a tick collar containing amitraz might be your best choice. For it to be most effective, though, it needs to fit properly. You should be able to get two fingers between the collar and your dog's neck. Cut off any extra portion so that he won't chew it.

A tick collar will kill ticks in less than 24 hours, and since it usually takes 48 hours to transmit a disease, you and your dog are probably home-free.

Worms

The sad fact is that most dogs get intestinal parasites sooner or later. Worms can do serious damage to your Weim's insides.

Roundworms, Hookworms, and Whipworms

Roundworms (*Toxocara canis*) are probably the most common intestinal parasite of dogs. The eggs are excreted in faeces and are spread when a dog comes in contact with them or the ground. (Oddly, fresh faeces are not infective, so it's important to get rid of them before they become so.) Roundworms also are transmitted across the placenta to puppies before they're born. Adult roundworms live in the dog's intestine, where they lay their many, many eggs. Roundworm infection causes diarrhoea, vomiting, and the characteristic potbelly seen in many puppies. They cause severe dehydration in puppies as well. Female roundworms can grow up to 7 inches (15 cm) in length—this is not something that you want in your dog!

Hookworms and whipworms attach to the intestinal lining and suck the blood of the infested dog. Both can cause severe anaemia. Your veterinarian can diagnose roundworms, hookworms, and whipworms by faecal examination. She can administer a single medication that will get rid of all three at once. (Most of this stuff works by anaesthetising the worm so that it releases its grip on the dog's guts and passes through his system.)

Tapeworms

Tapeworms are oddballs. Unlike most other parasites, they aren't contracted directly from the soil or from faeces. Dogs get tapeworm when they swallow a secondary carrier—which is usually a flea but could also be a rodent. Once the worm arrives inside the intestines, it grows quite large and feeds on the digesting material present there.

Tapeworms are often discovered by the owner when she sees what look like rice grains in the faeces. These are actually segments of the worms that break off periodically. Inside them are the eggs that become new little tapeworms.

Tapeworm isn't usually a big deal to a dog, but they can be irritating or even make the animal lose weight. Your vet can prescribe a medication that will get rid of them. Unfortunately, the same medication that kills hookworms, whipworms, and roundworms doesn't work on tapeworms.

Heartworms

A heartworm is a parasite (*Dirofilaria immitis*) that lives in the pulmonary vessels of the heart, or in severe cases, the heart itself. An individual worm can grow up to 1 foot long. As the worms multiply, they can cause high blood pressure, difficulty breathing, and heart failure.

Heartworms are spread by mosquitoes. (More than 70 different species have been implicated.) When the mosquito feeds on the blood of an already infected animal, an immature form of the worm, called microfilaria, gets sucked up into the mosquito. The microfilariae are

Sometimes roundworms are transmitted to puppies before they are born.

incubated inside the mosquito for several weeks, at which time they reach the infective stage and enter a new host when the mosquito bites again. They can spend up to five months maturing in the dog's body before migrating to the pulmonary arteries. Once the worms reach the pulmonary arteries, they grow and reproduce. Dogs may have heartworm for several years before signs of the disease appear.

Signs of heartworm include coughing, fainting, fatigue, and

difficulty breathing. However, these clinical signs may not show up for years after the animal has been infected. At this point, treatment can be quite dangerous—although without it the dog will certainly die.

By the time signs appear, the heart and pulmonary arteries are often so full of worms that treatment is very risky. The treatment for heartworm is a form of toxin administered at doses intended to kill the worms but not the dog. There is a risk that the animal may die during the process because the worms can choke the arteries as they begin to die off.

Whilst heartworm is rare in the UK, if you are travelling overseas with your dog you will need to discuss a preventative with your vet.

Prevention is much better than cure, and the good Weim owner will take advantage of oral preventives. These kill the worms before they have a chance to become adults. However, the preventive should be given to your pet *only* after a negative heartworm test has been done. Otherwise, a potentially life-threatening shock reaction could occur. Besides, the preventive will not kill the adult worms that are already present in the body, so the worms will continue to reproduce and grow.

PROBLEMS AND CONDITIONS IN THE WEIMARANER

While Weims are generally a healthy breed, they are prone to some problems and conditions.

If you are travelling abroad with you Weim, talk to your vet about Heartworm preventative.

Bloat

Bloat is a deadly condition that is all too common in Weimaraners. In fact, of all breeds, Weimaraners are the third most likely to develop this horrifying condition, right after Great Danes and St. Bernards. Bloat may be caused by overeating, but no one yet completely understands what brings it about in any given case. However, anatomy seems to play a critical role, and unfortunately, the deep-chested American-bred Weimaraner has exactly the right kind of anatomy for this condition to develop. In Germany, where Weims tend not to be so deep chested as in the United States, the condition is much less prevalent. Better breeding could lessen the incidence of the disease in the US as well.

In the most serious form of the condition, called gastric dilation volvulus, or GDV, the stomach swells and then twists. Because the dog's tummy is firmly attached only at one place near the top, it can easily rotate when it becomes full. The resulting painful condition damages the lining of the stomach and blocks blood flow to the heart, putting the dog into shock. Mortality rates are very high.

If your Weim suddenly develops a distended belly, paces, tries to vomit unsuccessfully, or seems in pain and is getting worse, get him to an emergency vet immediately. GDV is a life-threatening condition, and prompt decompression is required to relieve pressure on his blood vessels and heart. The most important thing to remember is *do not wait* to rush your dog to the vet. Don't fool around by trying over-the-counter medications—*take your dog to the vet.* Think of it this way—if it's *not* bloat, you're out the price of a vet visit. If it is, and you wait, your dog will die. What's more important? Don't play the odds. See the vet and *suggest* bloat. Some vets do not know that Weims are *very* prone to this killer disease.

The key is prompt, correct treatment. Dogs who are properly treated have a higher than 80 percent probability of surviving a bloat episode and then leading a normal life. But half of the dogs who die with a rotated stomach will do so before veterinary help is obtained.

Many clinical reports from Europe and the United States show that gastropexy, a procedure in which the stomach is attached to the body wall to prevent gastric rotation, should be performed as soon as possible following stomach decompression on all dogs with gastric dilatation. The recurrence rate of GDV in dogs treated without surgery approaches 100 percent, while the recurrence rate following gastropexy is less than 5 percent. The stomach of a dog who has had

Worms—Yuck!

Because Weimaraners are such outdoor-loving dogs, they need special attention paid to whether they have contracted internal parasites (worms). There are many types of worms that can enter their bodies through a variety of ways, and you may not even know that your dog has them. That's why it's important to maintain our veterinary visits an keep up to date with preventative worming programmes.

gastropexy can still dilate, but it is unlikely to rotate.

A dog's chance of developing GDV increases with age; dogs more than seven years of age are twice as likely to bloat as two year olds. Males are at higher risk than females, as are nervous and fretful dogs. To reduce your dog's chances of getting bloat, feed smaller and more frequent meals. Three meals a day is better than two. Statistics suggest that adding a few tablespoons of healthy table scraps to a dog's kibble may reduce the chances of him developing bloat. Another precaution is always to keep a product with simethicone on hand (like Mylanta); in fact, it wouldn't hurt to give your Weim a tablet with every meal. Another way to help to prevent bloat is to avoid exercising your dog right after a meal.

Blockages

Like many other hunting breeds, Weimaraners have a habit of eating untoward things, including dirt, tissues, and squeaky toys. Sometimes these objects are outright poisonous. At other times, they can form an obstruction in the intestine.

Deep-chested breeds like the Weimaraner are prone to bloat.

The main way to diagnose an obstruction is by taking X-rays of the abdomen. The vet is looking not just for lost screwdrivers and missing forks but also for abnormal areas of gas in the intestine that may show up better than the object itself. In some cases, the vet can administer barium orally, which is like a "white dye" that coats everything in the stomach and intestine and makes it appear white on an X-ray. It's not only sharp objects that are dangerous—even string can make the intestine bunch up and eventually cause a perforation. If this happens, septic peritonitis can result and kill the dog. Any intestinal blockage is an emergency.

If you're lucky, the foreign object can be retrieved via an endoscope and grasping tool without surgery, but sometimes an entire section of the intestine must be removed.

Blood Diseases

Weimaraners are subject to two different but similar inherited clotting diseases: von Willebrands disease (also known as Factor VIII Deficiency or

Hemophilia A) and Factor XI Deficiency. Dogs with von Willebrands have a slowed clotting. Factor XI deficiency is generally considered a more minor bleeding disorder but can be severe after surgery or trauma.

Both these problems are similar to haemophilia in people.

These are inherited diseases with no cure (as with people), so affected dogs must be monitored carefully. It's very important to let your vet know if your dog seems to be a "bleeder." Signs that your dog may be affected include obvious bleeding without an apparent cause, pale gums, bruises in the absence of trauma, tiny red spots in the whites of the eyes or gums, and blood in the stool or urine. Your vet can order a coagulation test to see if problems are present.

Bone and Joint Problems

Of course, Weimaraners need a lot of exercise to stay in good shape. But with such large, active dogs, owners should be particularly mindful of not stressing their pets' bones and joints.

Arthritis

Arthritis is the degradation of cartilage surrounding the bone, causing joint pain, stiffness, and reduced range of motion. It affects dogs of all ages because trauma and hip dysplasia can also produce it. In fact, large sporting breeds like Weims are at considerable risk because of all the athletics that their humans sometimes expect of them. Once arthritis begins, it will gradually worsen. While there is no cure for the disease, it can be treated and managed. Your dog's diet, his weight, and his level of activity all can be customised to reduce the pain and inconvenience of the disease.

If your dog has developed arthritis, the best way to help him is to keep him from strenuous games. Swimming, however, is a wonderful alternative. Lead walking also is good for your arthritic dog.

Nonsteroidal anti-inflammatory drugs (NSAIDS) can help to reduce the pain, although some dogs suffer from their side effects. Side effects to watch for include vomiting, reluctance to eat, tarry or bloody diarrhoea, lethargy, yellowish gums, increased thirst and urinating, bruising or speckling of the skin, behavioural changes, and dermatitis. Any of these signs should be reported at once. Talk to your vet about the best pain management for your dog. (Other therapies that can help to reduce the pain and inflammation of arthritis include exercise, physical therapy, omega-3 fatty acids, acupuncture, cold compresses,

These large, active dogs oftentimes stress their bones and joints.

and chondroprotectants.)

Hip Dysplasia

The word "dysplasia" means abnormal growth. Hip dysplasia is a progressive, developmental problem of young dogs (6 to 18 months of age) that shows up as chronic osteoarthritis. Dogs with hip dysplasia have a poor fit of the "ball and socket" hip joint. Normally, this joint consists of the round femoral head and the acetabulum or socket, plus the joint capsule and lubricating fluid. Dogs with hip dysplasia have "loose hips." The disease is caused partly by heredity and partly by nutritional factors, such as feeding a Weim puppy food designed for smaller dogs or by oversupplementing.

Dogs with hip dysplasia seldom cry or whine in pain, but they will exhibit reduced activity as well as difficulty rising or lying down or going up stairs. In some cases, a veterinarian can detect loose hips, but X-rays provide the definitive diagnosis of this disease. A diagnosis is very important for dogs who may be used as breeding stock. It is also of interest to the average pet owner who is concerned about possible hip disease in her Weimaraner.

In Weimaraners, hip dysplasia now occurs in only 8 percent of dogs because of conscientious breeding.

The British Veterinary Association and Kennel Club have joined forces to set up a screening scheme to detect the presence of hip dysplasia.

Hypertropic Osteodystrophy

Hypertropic osteodystrophy is a condition in which the bones, especially the long bones of the legs, grow too rapidly. The joints are swollen and painful. While the disease is more commonly associated with giant breeds, Weims are highly at risk. Genetics and oversupplementation of a puppy's food with calcium are risk factors. The disease generally strikes puppies between the ages of three and seven months, during the period of most rapid growth. Luckily, most puppies recover in a few weeks, although a few experience permanent bone deformities.

Ruptured ACL

The anterior cruciate ligament prevents the knee joint from bending the wrong way; it also prevents the joint from rotating or the tibia from sliding forward. A ruptured anterior cruciate ligament is a common and painful injury among both human and canine athletes. Fortunately, there is a new surgical procedure to treat this condition, which would otherwise lead to a permanent and disabling arthritis. When the ligament ruptures, the joint becomes unstable and the femur (the big thigh bone) can move freely over the tibia, which can tear the joint capsule of the knee. Your vet can usually diagnose the problem by checking for abnormal mobility in the joint as well as by observing the dog move. A patented new surgical procedure, called "tibial plateau leveling osteotomy" (TPLO) has been developed to stabilise the leg and prevent further degenerative changes in the joint. Dogs who undergo the procedure show improvement almost immediately.

Cancer

Dogs get cancer at roughly the same rate as humans, and cancer accounts for almost half of the deaths of dogs over ten years of age. In fact, it is the number-one cause of natural death among dogs. Forty-five percent of all dogs will get cancer, and it can occur in almost any part of the body and in any organ. Weimaraners are quite prone to cancers of various sorts.

Cancer occurs when cell

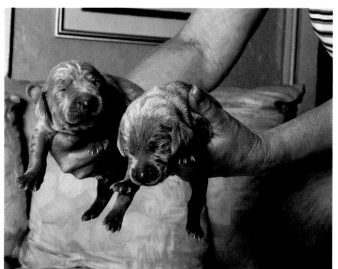

Good breeding has helped reduce the incidence of hip dysplasia in Weimaraners.

Degenerative Joint Disease

Degenerative joint disease (DJD) affects the articular cartilage. In healthy dogs, the joint cartilage works like a shock absorber and also provides a slippery surface for joint motion. However, sometimes secondary to an injury like a torn ACL or other health problem like arthritis, the joint can stop working properly. The most common sign is periodic lameness. Treatment depends on the severity of the disease. Options include rest, anti-inflammatory drugs, supplements to protect the cartilage, and moderate, regular exercise like lead walks and swimming. It's also important to keep your Weim trim. In some cases, surgical procedures like total hip replacement, removal of a portion of the bone (arthroplasty) and fusion of the joint (arthrodesis) may be necessary.

growth goes awry. For some reason we don't fully understand, an error has occurred in the DNA code to allow uncontrolled cell growth. In some cases, the error is minor, resulting in what doctors call a benign growth. If the changes are major and deleterious, it is called cancer or a malignancy. Your vet can examine a bit of tumour tissue in a biopsy to tell if it is benign or malignant. Tumours that come from glandular cells are called adenocarcinoma, while tumours arising in epithelial tissue are carcinomas. Those that arise from the skin, muscle, bone, and connective tissue are called sarcoma. When a tumour spreads from one area to another it is called metastatic. (Only malignant tumours do this, and when it happens, it is life threatening). Most horribly, cancer cells are "immortal," meaning that they don't die off when they should. They also seem to have the unlimited ability to reproduce themselves.

It is not known why some dogs get cancer and some don't. Heredity is one factor. So are things in the environment, like noxious chemicals, radiation, overexposure to the sun, and asbestos. Certain hormones seem to increase the chances of cancer, which is one reason why it's important to get your Weim spayed or castrated.

Signs of Cancer

Signs of cancer are often general and nonspecific, including weight loss, low-grade fever, lethargy, and weakness. A vet may diagnose tumours by palpation, X-ray, and biopsies; larger facilities may have CT scans, or MRIs. As an owner, look for:

- a lump or mass that increases in size
- a sore that does not heal
- change in toileting patterns, including difficulty urinating or defecating
- bleeding or discharge from any body opening
- loss of appetite and weight loss
- difficulty breathing
- persistent lameness or stiffness
- offensive odour
- difficulty swallowing

Common Cancers and Tumours

The most common tumours in dogs are skin cancers, and Weimaraners are particularly vulnerable. Melanomas, lipomas, basal cell tumours, and mast cell tumours are the most frequent. Ask your vet to examine all the lumps or masses that she observes in your dog.

Approximately 30 percent of all tumours found in dogs occur on the skin. Skin cancers come in various types. Papillomas are small, cauliflower-like viral tumours that proliferate as a dog ages. The vast majority is not malignant and cause no damage beyond being nicked or worried into bleeding by the dog as he grooms. Not all lumps on a dog's skin are cancer! Mastocytomas or mast cell tumours, the most common kind, are oval, firm, and slightly raised. (The normal mast cell is part of a defence mechanism that causes hives in response to an allergen.) Most mast cell tumours are only locally invasive, just affecting the skin, but they also can spread to other parts of the body. If they are caught early, they usually can be excised surgically with no further problems to the dog. Weimaraners have a fairly high incidence of this type of cancer.

Older unspayed females have a high incidence of mammary cancer. This cancer is caused by the hormone progesterone. Fifty percent of all breast tumours in dogs are somewhat malignant but are well encapsulated and easy to remove. Spaying females before their first or second heat cycle can prevent these tumours.

Lymphatic tumours, also called "lymphosarcomas" or "lymphomas," are common. They appear as solid growths that begin in the lymph nodes or bone marrow or as individual cells circulating in the blood (leukaemia). Lymphoma can attack the digestive system and liver, resulting in lethargy, vomiting, and diarrhoea, and in the case of the liver, a yellow tinge to the gums and skin. It also can affect the lungs, producing coughing and difficulty breathing. Lymphoma in dogs responds well to chemotherapy, and dogs receiving treatment may live for another couple years.

Oral tumours are common in older dogs and often begin bleeding by the time they are noticed. Most of them are highly malignant and include squamous cell carcinomas, adenocarcinomas, fibrosarcomas, and malignant melanomas. Unfortunately, they are very hard to remove entirely by surgery, although a large portion can be removed and then the dog treated with radiation. (Chemotherapy has not been very successful for most dogs with oral tumours.)

Abdominal tumours are common but are often not discovered until they are advanced. They include haemangiosarcoma, mast cell tumours, lymphoma, and prostate cancer. Weight loss, weakness, pale gums, protracted vomiting, continual diarrhoea, and abdominal enlargement may be signs.

An Anti-Cancer Diet

If your dog has been diagnosed with a cancerous tumour, a proper "anti-cancer" diet can help. The best diet is low in carbohydrates, high in protein, and high in fat, especially those all-important omega-3 fatty acids. The reason for this is that cancer cells prefer to use carbohydrates as an energy source rather than proteins or fats. Special veterinary commercial anti-cancer diets are available, but you also can cook up something special for your Weim at home that fits the bill. The diet should be about 50 percent fish or poultry and 50 percent vegetables. Add a couple teaspoons of olive oil, a vitamin/mineral supplement, and a calcium supplement.

Checking your Weim over for lumps and bumps is always a good idea.

Haemangiosarcoma is a malignant tumour of blood vessel cells; it can arise from any tissue where there are blood vessels. Dogs of any age are vulnerable, although it occurs most often in dogs who are eight years of age and older. Common sites include the skin, spleen, and heart. About 80 percent of them begin in the spleen, a large organ in the abdomen that stores blood. Haemangiosarcoma is very serious, although the skin form of the disease can sometimes be eradicated with surgery. (This form often appears as rosy red or black growths on the skin.) It often causes serious internal bleeding and spreads quickly. A dog may experience sudden weakness, pale gums, or even collapse. In other cases, the tumour grows more slowly without causing bleeding. The abdomen will become distended. In either case, surgery is indicated, often with chemotherapy. On average, however, treatment can add only about four months to the dog's life. Good veterinary care sometimes can achieve a remission; the type of haemangiosarcoma often determines the outcome. When haemangiosarcoma occurs on the skin, it often can be stopped because these types of tumours usually don't spread to other sites. Other types are rarely curable.

Osteosarcoma is a fast-spreading cancer that may begin at the growth plates near the ends of the long bones of the legs. Osteosarcoma develops deep within the bone, becoming more painful as it grows outward; the bone is destroyed from the inside out. The first sign to the owners is often a limp that may stay constant for one to three months. In later stages, it may metastasize to the lungs, and the dog may cough. The exact cause of osteosarcomas is unknown.

Males, uncastrated/unspayed dogs and large breeds, appear to be at the highest risk. The best treatment for these tumours is the removal of the affected leg. This sounds bad, but losing one leg in four does not substantially restrict your dog's activity level. In some cases, though, there is another option. The tumourous bone can be removed and either replaced by a bone graft from a bone bank, or the remaining bone can be regrown via a new technique called "bone transport osteogenesis." The joint nearest the tumour is fused. Chemotherapy drugs, along with radiation, are helpful when the tumour is inoperable. Radiation can be applied to the tumour in three doses (the first two doses one week apart followed by the third dose two weeks later). You can explore these options with your veterinarian.

All dogs with cancer should have good nutritional support because "cancer cachexia" stops many patients from eating. A dog with cancer should be on a tasty, energy-dense diet that is rich in fat and protein. Carbs should be kept to a minimum. (Cancer cells can't use fat very well but thrive on carbohydrates.)

Canine Cancer Care

Veterinary cancer specialists usually combine only three drugs for an effective therapy, compared to the ten or so that are typical for humans. This allows the dog to go into remission with minimal side effects and an excellent quality of life while the remission lasts, which is typically for many months.

There are many treatments available for dogs diagnosed with cancer.

Help in Detecting Disease

An early detection system called TRAP (Telomeric Repeat Amplification Protocol) used in the early detection of cancer in humans is now used for dogs. The test works by detecting the enzyme telomerase, which helps cancer cells reproduce indefinitely. Normal cells do not usually produce telomerase.

Ear Problems

A Weimaraner's ears are susceptible to a variety of medical problems, including infections and mites.

Ear Infections

Bacterial or yeast infections of the ear are extremely common. Infections can occur in the outer part of the ear canal *(otitis externa)*, the middle ear *(otitis media)*, or the inner ear *(otitis interna)*, with the first being the most common, especially in lop-eared dogs like Weimaraners. They can be sudden or chronic, but both conditions damage the lining of the ear canal. In about 70 percent of chronic cases, the eardrum ruptures. If the infection goes on for any length of time, the ear canal becomes scarred, calcified, and narrower in size. At that point, surgical intervention may be necessary.

In some cases, the infection might be precipitated by a tumour, foreign bodies like grass seeds, reactions to certain drugs, autoimmune disease, or even ear mites. Signs of outer and middle ear infection include:

- head shaking and scratching at the ears
- red or inflamed ears
- foul odour
- black or yellow discharge

Dogs who have an inner ear infection may tilt their heads and lose their balance. Their pupils may be of unequal size. Dogs with ear infections are miserable and need immediate attention.

If you suspect an infection, take your dog to the vet for an examination. She will inspect his ears with an otoscope, which gives a good view of the ear canal. She'll check, among other things, to see if the eardrum is intact. In serious cases, sedation or even anaesthesia must be used. The next step is usually an examination of cells that are causing the infection to determine their type. Often more than one type of bacteria or fungus is present. The results will tell what medication is best.

If your Weim has chronic or recurrent infections, there may be an underlying condition such as allergies or a low thyroid function. This condition will have to be addressed before her ears will be permanently free from infection.

In some cases, the dog's ear canal may be closed. Sometimes a medication can help; other times, surgery is necessary. In the most serious cases, the entire ear canal is removed, an operation that requires a specialist because severe scarring and calcification can occur.

Ear Mites

Ear mites are tiny, just barely visible to the naked eye as a white dot. However, they leave a characteristic discharge that looks like coffee grounds, a discharge that comprises earwax, blood, inflammatory biochemicals, and the ear mites themselves. They are transmitted by physical contact, so if one household pet (cat or dog) has them, the others probably do as well. Ear mites can produce an irritating infection in the ears. Your vet can prescribe a topical or injected medication to get rid of them.

Dogs who have an inner ear infection may tilt their heads. (Luckily this dog is just happy.)

Eye Problems

Weims are prone to two specific eye conditions. (For general canine eye problems, see section in "Other Problems and Conditions.")

Corneal Dermoid Cysts

Weimaraners are subject to cysts on the cornea. They may affect one or both eyes. This condition is hereditary in Weimaraners, but the mode of inheritance is unclear. If your dog is affected, discuss options with your vet.

Double Eyelashes

Dogs with this condition (also known as distichiasis) have an extra row of eyelashes that are usually, but not always, located on the lower part of the eyelid. This can cause tearing and irritation to the cornea, and it occurs frequently in Weimaraners. If your dog is affected, discuss options with your vet.

Hypomyelinogenesis

Hypomyelinogenesis, or delayed myelination, occurs in only six breeds, including Weimaraners. Some Weims are born with insufficient covering (myelin sheathing) over their nerves, and the dogs are

consequently uncoordinated and tremble. However, the prognosis is good, with most puppies recovering on their own at the myelin grows. Affected dogs usually become completely normal by the time they are one year old.

Skin Cysts

Weimaraners are subject to skin (dermoid) cysts that contain skin, glands, and hair. It is an inherited condition, although the mode of inheritance is still unclear. In this disease the "sinus" or cyst is lined with skin and may connect to the subarachnoid space in the spine, causing possible meningitis or myelitis. Veterinarians usually treat this problem with antibiotics and surgical excision of the sinus.

OTHER PROBLEMS AND CONDITIONS

Dogs also can develop problems that are not specifically breed related.

Addison's Disease (Hypoadrenocortisism)

The adrenal gland is located just in front of the kidney. It produces hormones called "corticosteroids." These hormones help to adapt an organism physiologically to stress, notably by producing the "fight-or-flight" impulse. In dogs with Addison's disease (hypoadrenocorticism), a deficiency of these hormones occurs. The most common victims are young (four to five years old) females. The first signs are listlessness, possibly with vomiting or diarrhoea. However, this can quickly turn into an "Addisonian crisis" in which the dog collapses and the blood sugar drops to a dangerous level, while potassium levels soar and disrupt the heart rhythm. Obviously, this can kill a dog. The only way to definitively diagnose Addison's disease is the ACTH stimulation test. ACTH is a pituitary hormone that actually releases the adrenal hormones.

Luckily, Addison's disease can be controlled by administering corticosteroids. The most common treatment is a drug called "DOCP" given about every 25 days.

Allergies

Practically any substance on earth can cause an allergy in a susceptible animal. The culprit is often, but by no means always, some sort of protein. The worse kind of allergic reaction is anaphylactic shock. (This is discussed in the first-aid section of this chapter.) It is life

threatening but thankfully quite rare. Most of the time, this reaction comes from a substance injected directly into the skin—a drug, vaccine, or insect sting.

Signs of allergy include:

- facial itching
- foot or leg chewing
- belly itching
- recurrent ear infections

Other reactions to allergens (usually insect stings) include uticaria, or small bumps in the skin. Sometimes the hair in the bumps stands up straight. Sometimes they are itchy. Angiodema is a facial swelling, especially around the eye and muzzle. Hives is another word for these bumpy swellings. They often appear within 20 minutes after exposure and usually go away on their own, although dogs with severe facial swelling may have problems breathing. Contact your vet for instructions should your dog experience hives. Your dog may be at risk for a more serious reaction if stung again.

One of the most common causes of allergies is flea saliva. In susceptible pets, even one flea bite can result in a severe allergic reaction.

Not all dogs exhibit all these signs. An allergy can not only be an annoyance, but it also can be dangerous because the skin is a protective organ. Once it is damaged, it can let in dangerous bacteria.

Aural Haematoma

A dog who shakes his head a lot due to an ear infection (or a wound) may rupture a blood vessel in the ear, causing bleeding into the tissues of the earflap or pinna. This is an aural (ear) haematoma. If it is serious, the dog may need surgery to remove the blood clots and have the ear cleaned and bandaged under anaesthesia. Surgery may not be needed in less serious cases, although the ear may look strange ever after.

Allergies can be caused by many different substances.

Seasonal Allergies

Spring is the high season for most allergies. If your dog has a tendency toward allergies, they will probably show up in your Weim between the ages of one and three years. (Flea allergic dermatitis, another major cause of seasonal itchiness, tends to begin later, between the ages of three and five.) Although most allergic substances are inhaled, your dog will respond not by sneezing the way you do but with the itchy skin problems described earlier. Your Weim also might develop skin or ear infections. This kind of allergy is often called atopy or allergic inhaled dermatitis. Common inhaled allergens are ragweed, pollen, house dust,

Spring is the high season for most allergies.

house dust mites, mould, animal dander, feathers, grasses, trees, and shrubs. The allergens can be inhaled, passed through the pads of the feet, and even possibly ingested. Because these compounds are in abundance everywhere, preventing exposure is impossible.

The best treatment for seasonal allergies is hyposensitisation or immunotherapy (allergy injections). When given periodic injections of small amounts of an allergen, your Weim gradually will become less sensitive to it. However, this therapy may take a year to become effective. It doesn't work with every dog, either. Because allergies tend to exacerbate each other, controlling one allergen, like fleas, may reduce the bad effects of other allergens. It certainly won't hurt.

In cases where hyposensitisation is not pos   (many dogs with seasonal allergies are allergic to practically ev   ig and don't respond), your vet may wish to resort to p   ne. A high dose is used in the beginning, but this is quickly   ed down. Safer but less effective treatments include antihistami: s, fatty acid supplements, and topicals.

Food Allergies

Food allergies occur when the proteins that your dog ingests are not recognised by the immune system as the "right ones." While many people think that a food allergy is due to a sudden change in diet, the opposite is often true. Food allergies usually take time to develop, meaning that your Weim may have been eating the allergenic protein for years without an obvious reaction.

To determine if your dog has a food allergy, a vet will place him on a hypoallergenic diet for a certain period. The traditional method is to use "novel" protein and carbohydrate sources—in other words, something that the dog has never eaten before. Venison, duck, or fish and potato are common choices. If the dog recovers, the original diet is resumed to see if the allergy comes back. If it does, the vet will know that it is something in the original food. The dog may stay on the hypoallergenic diet or be put on a different commercial diet. Recently, though, a new approach has been tried: developing diets made from "hydrolyzed proteins." This diet uses a conventional protein source in which the protein is broken down into molecules too small to stimulate the immune system. Talk to your vet about your choices.

Canine Flu

Canine flu is a new and highly contagious infection that is spreading across the United States. Originally, it was thought to be just another, worse kind of kennel cough, but it is now recognised as a separate disease that first appeared in racing Greyhounds. Because this disease is new, dogs have no natural immunity. Some animals show signs no worse than those of kennel cough, but others become very ill, even developing pneumonia. The death rate is between 1 and 10 percent, with dogs receiving supportive care most likely to recover. This is the first time that an influenza virus has been linked to respiratory disease in dogs. The virus originally migrated from one that affects horses.

Cardiovascular Problems

A canine's cardiovascular system requires the same type of good care that a human's

Heart Failure

When the heart is not able to pump the volume of blood it receives or can't pump out enough blood to supply oxygen to the body, heart

Diagnosing Allergies

Diagnosing the cause of an allergy may be difficult (some dogs have many allergies) and can involve taking a blood sample for analysis or intradermal testing, where numerous allergens are injected just under the skin and a reaction is noted at 15 minutes and again at 30 minutes. If the reaction is positive, it will produce a wheal, a hive-like swelling of the skin.

Heart Help

Try adding an omega fatty acid supplement to your Weim's diet if he is experiencing heart problems.

failure occurs. Heart failure can be an acute emergency, but often it's just a sign of an ageing dog. While there is no real cure, your vet can do a lot to make your dog more comfortable and to give him good quality of life.

The first step is sodium restriction. You can provide a veterinary-prescribed low-sodium diet, although many are so bland that dogs aren't eager to eat them. Sometimes you can mix in a salt-free treat that will encourage your pet. In other cases, you may have to resort to a veterinary diet made for kidney patients that are slightly higher in salt but more palatable to many pets.

You also must exercise your dog moderately—not so much that he pants. His days of relentless running are past.

Your vet may prescribe a diuretic, a drug that increases urine production. Furosemide is most commonly used, in combination with an ACE (Angiotensin Converting Enzyme) inhibitor for long-term therapy. ACE inhibitors result in less sodium retention and more open blood vessels. Some dogs also will receive digoxin in combination with these medications. Digoxin helps the heart pump better and keeps the heart beating smoothly and more slowly. Recent research also indicates that eplerenone, a novel selective aldosterone blocker, may be of help, but further studies are needed.

High Blood Pressure

Like humans, dogs can get high blood pressure, especially as they age. It can be caused by chronic renal failure, Cushing's disease, diabetes, and other conditions. High blood pressure can damage your dog's eyes and kidneys, and it increases the risk of embolism, or blood clots. If your Weimaraner is nine years old or older, be sure to ask your vet to check his blood pressure. If high blood pressure is present, your vet can treat both the underlying disease and the high blood pressure itself.

A canine's cardiovascular system requires the same type of good care that a human's does.

Patent Ductus Arteriosus (PDA)

PDA is the most common

congenital heart defect in dogs both large and small. The problem starts before birth, when a special passageway, the ductus arteriosus, does not close as it should. The hearts of dogs with this condition must work much harder to maintain a normal blood flow; in most cases, such dogs develop heart failure before they are two years old. Signs of the disease include coughing, rapid breathing, and exercise intolerance.

The good news is that PDA now can be repaired with a fairly simple, rather noninvasive procedure that blocks off the PDA using a device inserted through a catheter placed in a large vein.

Hope for Better Kidney Care

The most promising development in the search for early detection of kidney disease is a urine test that measures minute quantities of the protein albumin in urine. This test should be performed annually on all dogs aged seven years and older.

Chronic Renal Failure

Chronic renal failure is the most common kidney problem in dogs, but by the time one notices it, it is usually late in the disease process. This is because the kidneys are so efficient that 75 percent of the function can be lost before signs develop. Kidney failure can be congenital, genetic, acquired, or of unknown cause. The kidneys not only control water in the body but also help keep blood pressure in check, maintain electrolyte balance, and eliminate water-soluble products like urea. Early signs of renal failure include weight loss, irritability, poor coat condition, dehydration, and lethargy. Ulcers may form in the mouth. Your dog may drink and urinate more than usual, sometimes urinating in inappropriate places.

If your vet suspects chronic renal failure, she may suggest blood work or radiographs. Although it will worsen over time, good care can help. This may include IV fluid therapy, potassium supplementation, and a special low-protein, low-phosphate diet, now available commercially. Fish oils added to the diet also may be helpful. Medications showing promise in the treatment of kidney failure include ACE inhibitors like benazepril, which decrease the amount of protein shed in the urine.

Cognitive Dysfunction Syndrome (CDS)

Geriatric dogs are subject to most of the same ageing problems people have, and that includes a decline in mental powers. While some of this is common to ageing (although many dogs remain bright and alert until the end of a long life), there is a specific disease called cognitive dysfunction syndrome, or CDS, a disease markedly similar to Alzheimer's in human beings. The same type of changes in the brain occur, and many of the signs are similar, including disorientation, panting, increased sleeping, trouble figuring out stairs, confusion, and forgetfulness to the point of not even recognising members of the family. Dogs often regress in their housetraining, seem to seek solitude, or get "stuck" in a corner. Some dogs also start barking for no apparent reason.

The older a dog gets, the more likely he is to be a victim of the disease. However, a treatment (deprenyl or selegiline) is available that can reverse many of the signs of CDS. In fact, deprenyl has been shown to actually increase the life span of a dog! For more information, contact your veterinarian, who will want to give your dog a thorough examination. Remember that this is a disease—it's not "normal" for an older dog to experience dysfunction at this level.

Cushing's Disease

Cushing's disease occurs when the body produces too much cortisol, a steroid hormone produced by the adrenal glands that is critical for normal body function. In some older dogs, usually because of a tumour in the pituitary gland or even on the adrenal gland itself, excess cortisol is produced. Too much cortisol can reduce the ability of the kidneys to reabsorb water, so the dog tends to urinate more frequently and drink more water. The excess cortisol also seems to affect the appetite centre of the brain, which makes some dogs extremely hungry all the time.

When there's too much cortisol over a long period, the result is muscle wasting, fat redistribution, and an enlarged liver. Many dogs with Cushing's disease have a distinctive "pot-bellied" appearance. They also may lose hair symmetrically in the trunk area and have skin infections. (Too much cortisol suppresses the immune function.)

There are several available treatments for Cushing's. If the tumour is on the adrenal gland, it may be possible to remove it surgically.

Urinary Tract Infections and Bladder Stones

A number of factors can cause urinary infections in dogs—everything from bacteria overgrowth to bladder stones. Bladder stones form from a single irritating particle called a nidus. (They are sort of like pearls in a way.) This nidus collects a progressively larger coating of minerals that can, over time, become irritating to the lining of the bladder. If a bladder stone gets lodged in the urethra, it becomes difficult for the animal to urinate. If the vet suspects bladder stones, she will take an X-ray and perhaps do an ultrasound examination. Bladder stones come in several varieties, and it's important to determine the type of stone before treatment is begun. Some kinds can be dissolved with medication, while others, like ones made of calcium oxalate, cannot. These stones must be removed surgically.

In other cases, medications are available that can decrease, at least temporarily, the amount of cortisol produced. With good medical treatment, your dog's life span may be increased by 18 months—which can be a long time for a dog.

A change in your Weim's behaviour might indicate a medical problem—be sure to have him checked out with your vet.

Diabetes Mellitus

Both humans and dogs are subject to diabetes, an incurable, complicated, but treatable condition. Diabetes can occur at any age in dogs but is most frequently diagnosed between the ages of seven and nine. Female dogs are about twice as likely as male dogs to develop the condition. The disease comes in two types: Type I and Type II.

Type I is a condition in which the beta cells in the pancreas fail to release sufficient insulin, which helps to transport glucose to the cells where it is needed. Instead, the glucose stays in the blood, and the cells die. When the glucose builds up too much, it eventually leaks into the urine.

In Type II diabetes, the body becomes resistant to the effects of insulin or the beta cells are dysfunctional. This is the kind of diabetes that you see with obese patients (both human and animal).

Dogs can develop diabetes because of an immune dysfunction—

the dog's own antibodies attack the beta cells in the pancreas. It also can develop from pancreatitis or infections.

The main signs of diabetes are excessive thirst and urination. Some dogs are also constantly hungry but lose weight anyway. Your veterinarian will detect sugar in the urine, and the blood glucose will be elevated. Diabetic dogs can develop cataracts and are prone to urinary infections. (The extra glucose in the urine makes a home for bacteria.)

All diabetic dogs must receive insulin once or twice a day, a tricky process in itself. Too much insulin can make the dog hypoglycaemic (low blood sugar). If too little is given, the disease remains uncontrolled. When a dog's blood sugar gets too low, the dog can go into shock. This is why a correctly working pancreas is so important—it takes care of all these little details.

In the beginning, a diabetic animal may need to have his blood tested every couple hours to observe when the glucose peaks and declines in response to the insulin. (This is called a glucose curve.) Consistency and a restricted lifestyle that adhere to the following points are the keys to keeping a diabetic dog healthy:

Diabetes is a treatable condition.

- The amount and timing of exercise should be the same every day.

- The amount of food and feeding times should be the same every day. If the diabetes has progressed to the point where the dog is seriously underweight, a high-calorie diet may be needed until weight returns to normal.
- The amount and time of insulin given should be the same every day.
- Diabetic females should be spayed; the swinging hormone levels in unspayed dogs make the disease harder to control.

Eye Problems

Your dog's eyes are not only expressive—they also are delicate and subject to many diseases and injuries. Be aware of typical signs of eye problems, such as discharge, squinting, redness, and cloudiness. Call your vet if you notice them.

Cataracts

The lens of the eye is used to focus. It is completely clear and suspended in position by special tissue fibres ("zonulae") located just inside the pupil. Cataracts are defined as any opacity in the lens of the eye, and they usually occur in older animals. Causes include genetic predisposition, trauma, diabetes, and toxins. (They've also been known to occur following radiation therapy for cancer.)

Typically, a cataract gives the eye a cloudy appearance. Once a cataract has begun to form, it eventually will obscure vision completely. The only to way get rid of a cataract is through a surgical procedure to remove the lens. In some cases, a lens implant can be used, but even without it, a dog with a lens removed can see better than one whose lens is obscured by the cataract. (They just have trouble focusing on things that are very close.) In any case, even in healthy dogs, the focusing power of the lens is three times weaker than in people. Dogs could probably never read the fine print on their dog food labels.

Sometimes, long-standing cataracts can begin to dissolve. Although this sounds great, it isn't and in fact is a highly inflammatory process that can cause uveitis, a condition that is painful and can even lead to glaucoma.

It is safer, easier, and less expensive to remove a small, soft cataract than an old one, but surgery is not usually considered unless it can restore sight. In other cases, a cataract does not necessarily require treatment if there is no associated inflammation or glaucoma.

Inhalers for Dogs

Good news! Dogs may soon be able to safely receive insulin through a spray pump similar to an asthma inhaler, although right now the product is marketed only for humans — even though they tested it on dogs first.

"Cloudy" Eyes

As a dog gets older, the lens of the eye becomes more compact with zonulae, and the eye may appear a bit cloudy. This condition is called "nuclear sclerosis," but it is not the same as cataracts. Dogs with this condition can see through the lens, which is still clear.

Dogs with diabetes are particularly in danger of developing cataracts.

Cherry Eye

The healthy canine eye keeps itself moist through the use of two tear-producing glands, sort of like a windshield. One gland is located above the eye; the other is found within the dog's third eyelid (nictitating membrane). The gland sometimes "prolapses" outward and looks like a red mass or cherry. The proper treatment for the condition is to put the gland back where it belongs so that it can continue to keep the eye moist. (In the past, the gland was simply cut out, leading to dry eye and a host of problems.) There are several different surgical procedures to do this; they usually involve repositioning the gland.

Conjunctivitis

Conjunctivitis is the inflammation of the mucous membranes lining the eyelid and white part of the eye (sclera). It is the most common eye disease in dogs. What you are seeing is increased blood in the area, an inflammation usually caused by a virus or bacteria, although parasites or allergies also may cause it. There is often a clear or mucous discharge as well. Conjunctivitis is itchy, so your first job is to keep the eye clean and apply the prescribed medication, usually medicated ointment or drops.

Entropion

Entropion is a common hereditary disorder; it typically reveals itself in young dogs less than one year of age. Entropion means that the eyelids have rolled back and rub against the cornea, causing tearing and even vision loss. Your veterinarian can diagnose the disease by examining the eyelids, but some dogs also will show signs such as tearing, or reddening of the eye. It is common in many breeds and can be repaired surgically with a little nip and tuck. If left untreated, entropion can result in lifelong damage to the eyes.

Glaucoma

While both people and dogs can get glaucoma, there's an important difference. With people, the disease progresses slowly and often painlessly. With dogs, it often has a fast onset, is excruciatingly painful, and is a veterinary emergency. The disease is caused when the eye fluid (aqueous humour) does not drain properly; it builds up, causing pressure and damaging the optic nerve. Unfortunately, dogs are so stoic that you may not even know that your dog has the problem unless you are alert for its signs: squinting, redness, and cloudiness.

The vet will measure the eye pressure, and if necessary, begin emergency treatment. In cases where the pressure has been caused by some physical plugging of the "drain" in the eye, like a tumour, chronic uveitis, or lens luxation, sight may be restored. However, in the case of hereditary glaucoma, sight will usually be lost in both eyes. However, the disease still needs to be treated, sometimes requiring the removal of the blind eye, to stop the pain.

Keratoconjunctivitis Sicca (KCS)

KCS occurs when there is insufficient moisture in the eye. Dogs with this condition usually have a thick mucous discharge. Eventually, an ulcer may develop. Treatment involves tear stimulants and anti-inflammatory medication.

See your vet if you notice your Weim's eyes are irritated.

Scleritis

Scleritis is an inflammatory disease that effects the conjunctiva, sclera and episclera. It usually affects only one eye. A lumpy, hard red area may develop suddenly. It may be treated with steroids.

Uveitis

Uveitis is an inflammation of part or all of the uvea, which surrounds much of the eye with blood vessels. Affected animals have eye pain, tearing, eyelid spasm, and sensitivity to light. If left untreated, the dog's vision will be affected.

Hypothyroidism

Hypothyroidism is the most common hormone imbalance of the dog. Canines with this condition suffer from an inadequate production of the thyroid

Blindness

Dogs can live a normal life without vision. They can play and run, and they still enjoy their food, their naps, and being petted. They can memorise the layout of the furniture and don't seem in the least perturbed that someone has turned off the lights.

hormones. When the thyroid gland malfunctions, every cell in the body is affected. The hair becomes brittle, sparse, and coarse, and it's easily pulled out. The dog may be lethargic and his eyelids will droop. The average age for a dog to develop a low thyroid condition is between the ages of three and five; most cases are inherited. A blood test (for T4, the main thyroid hormone, and canine TSH, the thyroid-stimulating hormone from the pituitary gland) can detect the disease, and your vet will put your dog on an inexpensive thyroid supplement (L-thyroxine) as a lifelong treatment.

Inflammatory Bowel Disease

Inflammatory bowel disease is a condition in which cells involved in inflammation and immune response infiltrate the lining of the GI tract and disrupt its function. Signs include watery diarrhoea and chronic vomiting. The cause is not well understood. Your vet may diagnose the disease using a blood panel, X-ray, and urinalysis to rule out other problems. The definitive diagnosis is a biopsy.

The basic treatment is to suppress the inflammation using metronidazole or prednisone. In very severe cases, a stronger immunosuppressant may be needed. In addition, your Weim will be put on a fat-reduced, novel-protein ("hyperallergenic") diet that also contains increased nondigestible fibre, which increases faecal bulk and produces slower stool passage.

Hypothyroidism is usually an inherited condition.

Lyme Disease

Lyme disease is caused by the corkscrew-shaped spirochete *Borrelia burgdorferi*; it is spread by ticks of the *Ixodes* family, most notably the tiny deer tick. These ticks can be smaller than the head of a pin! It's important to remember that ticks are the transmitters, not the cause, of the disease. Lyme disease was first described in 1975 when there was an unusual outbreak of rheumatoid arthritis in children in Lyme, Connecticut. The disease can cause generalised illness in both animals and humans. Dogs are most frequently infected, but the disease also can occur in horses, cattle, and cats.

The most common sign of Lyme disease in

dogs is sudden lameness or arthritis. Other signs may include fever, lack of appetite, dehydration, lethargy, and swollen lymph nodes. Unlike people with Lyme disease, dogs will not develop a rash. A diagnosis is usually made based on a history of being in an endemic area, signs of

arthritis, and favourable response to treatment. Note: If your dog is diagnosed with Lyme disease, you are not at risk of getting it directly from your pet.

A blood test that measures antibodies to the bacteria is available. However, the test is not completely reliable, because many dogs who live in endemic regions will have a "positive" response to the test. It is not possible to know whether the dog had the disease or had just been exposed. In fact, in a Lyme endemic area, as many as 90 percent of dogs have antibodies against the Lyme spirochete. Most never become ill, but almost all of them will develop antibodies that persist for years and will show up as "positive" on most tests.

In the past, dogs who were vaccinated against Lyme also would show a "positive" response to a blood test. However, a new test, called the "C6 test," looks for a unique section of an antigen that is not present in the vaccine, so vaccinated dogs will not test positive. If the blood test shows positive, your vet may want to put your dog on a course of antibiotics just to be safe. Treatment must continue for a few weeks after all signs of the disease are absent from the dog. If the dog has the disease, it will almost always respond rapidly. If he doesn't, the therapy won't hurt him.

The best cure for Lyme disease is prevention. Using good tick control and early removal of the tick are important steps in this direction. Infected ticks must feed for about 24 hours to transmit the bacteria to its victim. The spirochete that causes Lyme disease cannot live outside the host's body. It must live inside either a mammal or a tick.

There is a vaccine approved for use in dogs with Lyme disease, but many experts recommend against vaccinating dogs in nonendemic areas. Its effectiveness is also a matter of debate. However, better, longer lasting vaccines against Lyme are being developed and marketed even now. Check with your vet for the latest developments.

Pancreatitis

Pancreatitis is the inflammation of the pancreas, and it can be life threatening. The pancreas helps with digestion and regulates blood

Use a good tick control to help prevent Lyme disease.

sugar. Pancreatitis is a common disease of dogs and generally occurs after a canine has eaten a high-fat meal, either a juicy steak or a selection from the rubbish bin. Note that it often occurs around holidays, when people keep handing out those "harmless" little tidbits to dogs.

With pancreatitis, the enzymes responsible for fat production are released prematurely and start to digest the cells of the pancreas itself. Signs include loss of appetite, vomiting, abdominal pain, and depression. In severe cases, it can be fatal. Take the dog to the vet for treatment.

Pneumonia

Probably the most well-known disease of the respiratory system is pneumonia, an inflammation of the lungs. There are many types of pneumonia, and it can have several causes: fungi, viruses, parasites, bacteria, and allergens. In most cases, however, no matter what the precipitating cause, bacteria are involved somehow. The definitive diagnosis for pneumonia is a chest X-ray (although the results can be hard to read). Signs include coughing, listlessness, fever, and appetite loss. Treatment includes IV fluids, antibiotics, and sometimes a therapy called nebulisation, in which a piece of specialised equipment sends a mist of saline droplets into the respiratory tract. A physical therapy technique called coupage, or cupping the hand over the chest and tapping it to release phlegm, is helpful. You can learn how to do this technique yourself.

Seizures

A seizure is a condition in which the neurons in the brain misfire. Causes may include trauma or infection within the brain, low blood sugar, or toxins. Often, however, no "cause" is found. This condition is called idiopathic epilepsy.

Seizures can last from 30 seconds to several minutes. They may be divided into generalised (grand mal) seizures that involve the whole body and partial seizures, which in turn may generalise to attack the whole body. A third form of seizure, the psychomotor seizure, is characterised by abnormal behaviour like snapping and circling; this may be followed by a generalised seizure.

Seizures often occur in stages. In the beginning, the dog may appear lost or restless. He may lick his lips, twitch, and seem nervous. During the actual seizure, he will lose consciousness, shake, and salivate excessively. Many lie on their side and make scrambling or paddling motions. Some dogs will defecate or urinate involuntarily. After the seizure is over, during the "post-ictal" period, the dog will appear dazed. Some press their heads against a wall, looking as if they have one heck of a headache.

During the seizure itself, there is little that you can do except keep the area dark, quiet, and free of things that your dog could strike during the episode. There is no first aid. In most cases, it is best to keep away from the dog because he could bite involuntarily, although I must confess that my seizure-prone dog, Clipper, seems to respond slightly when I speak quietly to him and stroke his back.

While short seizures are not really dangerous, long seizures can result in serious brain damage or even death. A seizure that lasts more than five minutes nonstop or more than three seizures within 24 hours is an emergency situation. Call your vet.

There are several medications, such as phenobarbital, that can help a dog with seizures. While phenobarbital is an inexpensive medication, its use requires frequent blood checks that can become costly. Talk to your vet. Most dogs with this condition can lead long and happy lives.

LAB TESTS AND DIAGNOSTIC IMAGING

While your vet has a keen eye, she can't always tell you what, if anything, is wrong with your dog by merely looking at and feeling him. Modern vets have at their disposal a plethora of tests that they can order to pinpoint an ailment and help your dog heal quickly.

Blood Cell Tests

A complete blood count (CBC) measures the number and types of cells circulating in the bloodstream. The three major types of blood cells are red blood cells, white blood cells, and platelets (cell fragments). Red blood cells are produced in the bone marrow, which is the soft centre of bones. They pick up oxygen from the lungs and distribute it to cells throughout the body. The CBC also measures

Web Help

For more information about epilepsy, information is available on the Internet.

There are several medications that can help with seizures.

haemoglobin, the substance in the red blood cell that carries oxygen. Decreased red blood cells produce the condition known as anaemia. Too many red blood cells usually suggest dehydration.

Another blood cell test is the packed cell volume (PCV), called "haematocrit" in humans. The PCV is the percent of red blood cells compared to the total volume of blood. In normal dogs and cats, 40 to 50 percent of the blood is made up of blood cells and the rest is fluid.

While there are several sorts of white blood cells, the most numerous are neutrophils, which help to fight infections. A low count of neutrophils may indicate bone marrow disease or a virus. A high level indicates inflammation or infection. Dogs on chemotherapy may have decreased numbers; dogs on cortisone treatment may have more. The other kinds of white blood cells are lymphocytes, monocytes, eosinophils and basophils. Lymphocytes are produced in the lymph nodes; the others all are produced in the bone marrow along with red blood cells. Lymphocytes also help to fight infection and produce antibodies against viruses and bacteria. A high level of them indicates infections, and low levels may indicate stress. Cortisone treatment also can decrease the number of lymphocytes. Increased levels of monocytes indicate a chronic infection, and increased levels of eosinophils or basophils suggest allergies or parasites.

Platelets are made in the bone marrow; they help blood to clot. Platelet destruction can be caused by bone marrow damage or certain diseases like immune-mediated thrombocytopenia. Dogs with a low platelet count bleed easily and may show blood in the stool.

Chemistry Panel Findings

When the veterinarian takes a blood sample, she may want to do a chemistry panel, which measures various substances in the blood. Too much or too little of a substance can reveal a problem. The blood panel may test the following:

- **Albumin:** Albumin is a small protein produced by the liver. It works like a sponge to hold water in the blood vessels. Albumin is decreased if the liver is damaged and cannot produce enough. Albumin also can be lost through damaged intestines or in the urine due to kidney disease. Increased albumin indicates dehydration.

- **Alkaline Phosphatase:** This enzyme originates from many tissues. High levels indicate liver disease or bone disease, although increased blood cortisol from drugs or Cushing's disease may also cause it.

- **ALT (SGPT) and AST (SGOT):** These liver-produced enzymes are increased if liver damage is present.

- **Amylase and Lipase:** Amylase is an enzyme produced by the pancreas and the intestinal tract; it helps to break down sugars. Increased levels may indicate pancreatitis or cancer of the pancreas. Lipase is a pancreatic enzyme that breaks down fats. Increased levels also may indicate pancreatitis or cancer.

- **Bile Acids:** Bile acids are produced by the liver to help break down fat. Dogs with abnormal blood flow to the liver will have abnormal levels of bile acids. Measuring bile acids requires two blood samples, one after fasting and the other two hours after eating.

- **Bilirubin:** Bilirubin is a waste product produced by the liver from old red blood cells. It is higher in dogs with certain kinds of liver disease, gallbladder disease, or in patients with haemolysis, a condition in which the red blood cells are destroyed at a faster than normal rate. Large amounts of bilirubin in the blood will give a yellow appearance in the tissues around the eye, inside the ears, and on the gums.

- **Blood Urea Nitrogen:** Blood urea nitrogen (BUN) is a waste product produced by the liver from proteins. It is normally eliminated from the body by the kidneys. A low BUN can be seen with liver disease, and an increased BUN is seen in pets

There are many tests your vet can perform to help discover problems in your dog.

with kidney disease. However, the kidneys must be damaged to the point that they are 75 percent nonfunctional before BUN will increase. Kidneys are pretty efficient.

- **Calcium:** Hormones cause bone to release calcium into the blood and then remove calcium from the blood and place it back into bone. It's a complex process. High blood calcium is most commonly associated with cancer, although it also can be caused by chronic kidney failure, primary hyperparathyroidism, poisoning, and bone disease. Low blood calcium results from a malfunction of the parathyroid glands, which produce a hormone (PTH) that controls blood calcium levels, or poisoning with antifreeze. There is also a condition called eclampsia in pregnant or nursing dogs that produces low levels of calcium, but this disease is most commonly seen in small dogs, not Weimaraners.

- **Cholesterol:** Cholesterol can be increased in dogs with hypothyroidism, Cushing's disease, diabetes, and kidney diseases that cause protein to be lost in the urine. However, the good news is that high cholesterol in dogs does not seem to produce heart and blood vessel disease the way it does in people.

- **Creatinine:** Creatinine is a waste product that originates from muscles and is excreted by the kidneys. High levels indicate kidney disease or dehydration. Its levels usually increase with the BUN if kidney disease is present.

- **Creatinine Kinase:** This is an enzyme that in elevated levels indicates damage to the muscle, including heart muscle.

- **Glucose:** Glucose is blood sugar. High levels indicate diabetes mellitus, and mildly increased levels are sometimes present in dogs with Cushing's disease. Low blood sugar signals pancreatic cancer or overwhelming infection.

- **Phosphorus:** Phosphorus is a mineral that comes from bones and is controlled by the same hormone, PTH (parathyroid hormone), that controls blood calcium. It is elevated in dogs with chronic kidney disease. Like BUN and creatinine, phosphorus increases following severe (more than 75 percent) kidney damage.

- **Potassium:** Higher than normal levels of this mineral indicate acute kidney failure, Addison's disease, or a ruptured or obstructed bladder.

- **Sodium:** High levels of sodium may indicate dehydration; low blood sodium is most commonly seen with Addison's disease.

- **Total Protein:** This test measures albumin and larger proteins called globulins. Total protein can be elevated with dehydration or if the immune system is being stimulated to produce large amounts of an antibody. Total protein is decreased if the dog has bowel or kidney disease. It also may be decreased if the dog has an abnormal immune system.

Urinalysis

Urine is more than a waste product—it's a clue to your dog's health. Odd as it sounds, there's lot that you can learn from dog urine. Healthy urine is a clear yellow with a characteristic dog-urine smell. (This cannot be described, only experienced.) Not only that, but a healthy dog will develop a particular pattern of urinating the same amount and frequency each day. A wise owner will note when the urination pattern changes or when the urine looks or smells different. When that happens, it may be time to collect a fresh (that's important—nobody wants your dog's old urine) sample and trot it off to your vet.

The concentration, colour, clarity, and microscopic examination of the urine sample can provide diagnostic information about several body systems. In some cases, you'll be responsible for collecting the urine. The easiest method is the old "free catch" method in which you take your dog for a walk and slip a clean plastic container underneath when he lifts his leg (or she squats—be thankful that you don't have a Dachshund). If you must wait for a period before going to the veterinarian, you can cover the container and keep it in the refrigerator for a short time.

Finding a good vet is one the best ways to keep your Weim healthy.

If for some reason you can't manage that, the urine can be collected at the clinic with a urinary catheter. In some cases, the vet may use cystocentesis, a procedure in which a needle is inserted directly into the bladder.

Your vet will check the sediment in the urine for increased white blood cells (possibly indicating a bladder infection, quite common in females). Diabetic dogs may have increased glucose in the urine. Bladder stones can give away their presence by leaving struvite crystals in the urine; ammonium biurate crystals signal liver problems.

Diagnostic Imaging

Today's vets can take advantage of many high-tech procedures to help to see what is going on with dogs. The most familiar of these procedures is the radiograph, or x-ray. The X-ray machine projects X-rays through the patient onto X-ray sensitive film. They pass through soft tissues easily but are blocked by bone. So on an X-ray, bones will appear clear, a cavity dark, and soft tissues grey.

Another tool is the CAT (computerised axial tomography) scan. Here, a very thin beam of X-rays passes through a cross-section of the body in a rotational manner. The beam can be adjusted to show very specific image slices, like showing the skull one section at a time. A computer also can use the scan to create a three-dimensional image. The CAT scan is very useful in determining subtle variations in tissue.

The MRI (magnetic resonance imaging) uses radio waves and powerful magnetic fields to create images. It creates a vibration in the fluid found in the body, which in turn emits a radio signal. A receptor coil produces a cross-sectional image of body water content found in the tissues. Bones are not shown (they contain too little water), but this imaging gives the best views of soft tissues like the liver or brain. Ultrasound uses high-frequency sound waves to detect problems in the heart, spleen, or liver, as well as the movement of foetuses.

All these diagnostic tools require special training, and many are expensive, cumbersome, and unsuited to an all-purpose veterinary practice, which may have only an X-ray machine.

Today's vets can take advantage of many high-tech procedures to help to see what is going on with dogs.

FIRST AID AND EMERGENCIES

Even though you aren't a vet, you can help your Weimaraner in an emergency. Follow these three easy-to-remember rules:

1. Be prepared—make up a first-aid kit and learn the common signs of trouble.

2. Be calm—panicky owners make the situation worse.

3. Protect yourself—even friendly dogs may bite if injured. Using a towel or t-shirt to cover the dog's eyes and applying a muzzle (handmade if you have to) will help. If you have leather gloves at hand, wear them.

Abrasions

An abrasion is a fancy word for a scrape. If the scrape is less than 1 inch (2.5 cm) in diameter, you can probably treat it at home. Wash your hands carefully and clip away the hair around the wound. (Use electric clippers if you have them.) Then flush the wound with saline solution or warm water to remove debris. Apply an antibiotic cream twice a day. If the would begins seeping pus or gets worse, call your vet.

Anaphylactic Shock

Anaphylaxis is a rare, life-threatening, immediate allergic reaction. It is almost always caused by something injected, such as stings, antibiotics, and vaccines, although it can happen (very rarely) with food or other agents in susceptible animals. Unfortunately, there's no way to predict what dog may have an anaphylactic reaction to what substances.

Signs include diarrhoea, vomiting, shock, seizures, and coma. The dog's gums will be pale and the legs cold to the touch. The pulse will be fast but weak. Unlike hives (another allergic reaction), there is no facial swelling. If untreated, it results in shock, respiratory and cardiac failure, and death. If your Weim is having such a reaction, get him to the vet immediately. Do not wait. He'll be treated with epinephrine, IV fluids, oxygen, and other medications.

Once you know that your dog is susceptible to something like bee stings, your vet will teach you how to give an injection yourself (perhaps with an epi-pen, a special syringe and needle filled with a single dose of epinephrine) and let you bring the medication home.

Drug Alert

Glucocorticoids (prednisone and prednisolone) are commonly prescribed medications, although few people know exactly how they work or even what they are. Glucocorticoids are hormones that break down stored fat, sugar, and proteins in the body to use in times of stress. They also are anti-inflammatory and immune-suppressive, and this is usually why they are prescribed. (The adrenal glands produce them naturally in the body.) Your vet may prescribe glucocorticoids for joint pain, itchy skin, cancer (especially for lymphoma), central nervous system disorders, shock (to improve circulation), and blood calcium reduction. They also can unmask hidden infections by depressing the immune system.

The drugs do have side effects, however, such as excessive thirst and urination. Higher doses can be irritating to the stomach. In addition, these drugs should not be used at the same time as Rimadyl or other NSAIDs; the combination could cause stomach ulcers. Diabetic and pregnant dogs should not take these medications. The medication also may change liver enzyme and thyroid blood testing.

When prednisone is prescribed for a long period of time, its use needs to be tapered off gradually, not suddenly stopped. Suddenly stopping the medication doesn't give the adrenal glands enough warning to start producing the normal amount of glucocorticoids on their own.

Knowing first aid can help keep your Weim safe.

Bleeding

If there is an obvious source of bleeding, stop it by pressing on the area (directly at the site of the wound) with a clean towel. Don't pull away the towel to "check" because you could pull away a scab that is forming. Get your dog to the vet.

Breathing Stops

CPR is an emergency technique used to help a person or animal whose heart or breathing has stopped. The purpose of the technique is to keep the patient alive until the heart begins beating on its own or a cardiac defibrillator can be used. Sadly, it is successful in only a small percentage of cases, even when performed by a skilled veterinarian. However, you have nothing to lose, and attempting CPR may save your dog's life!

CPR is as simple as ABC: *Airway, Breathing* and *Circulation,* in that order. Don't begin the technique unless you are sure that your dog is not breathing or has no pulse. It is dangerous if the animal is breathing on his own. Check for breathing by simply looking for the telltale rise and fall of the chest. Check for a pulse by placing your hand on the left side of the chest or on the inside of the thigh. (Dogs do *not* have a distinct neck pulse.)

Airway

Check to make sure the throat and mouth are clear. (Be careful; even a nonresponsive dog can bite automatically.) To clear the airway:

- Lay your dog on his side.
- *Slightly* tilt the head slightly back to extend the neck.
- Gently pull the tongue out of your pet's mouth.
- Reach carefully into the oral cavity to remove an obstruction or vomit.
- If necessary, perform the Heimlich manoeuvre.

Going Strong

Visit your veterinarian at the first sign of ill health. Prevention is the best medicine.

Breathing

To help your dog start breathing, perform the following "rescue" breathing technique:

- Straighten but don't overextend the neck.
- Perform mouth-to-nose breathing. Close the mouth and lips by placing your hand around the lips and holding the muzzle closed.
- Place your mouth over the dog's nose.
- Exhale forcefully four or five times. Give four or five breaths quickly.
- Check to see if breathing has resumed. If breathing hasn't begun or is shallow, begin rescue breathing again.
- Give about 20 breaths per minute. For puppies, give 20 to 30 breaths a minute.
- Check for a heartbeat. If no heartbeat is detected, begin cardiac compressions with rescue breathing. (See next step.)

Circulation

- Place the dog on his side on a hard surface.
- Kneel down next to the animal with his back near you.
- Extend your elbows and cup your hands on top of each other.
- Place your cupped hands over the ribs at the point where the raised elbow meets the chest.
- For an adult dog, compress the chest 2 to 3 inches at a rate of 1.5 to 2 times per second.
- Begin with five compressions for each breath. Check for a heartbeat after one minute and continue if you can detect none.

Broken Limbs

For a broken leg, immobilise the animal and get him to a vet. Don't try to set or even splint the limb. Just take your Weim to the vet right away. Most fractures result from pets being hit by a car, jumping from heights, or other trauma.

Constipation

One or two episodes of constipation are nothing to worry about. In fact, the intestines can store up an awful lot of stool without any ill consequences. However, recurrent bouts are worth checking out. With true constipation, the stools appear hard. Causes can include excessive

First-Aid Kit

Your first-aid kit should include the following:

- Antibiotic cream
- Benadryl—if approved by your veterinarian
- First-aid tape
- Gauze rolls and pads
- Hydrogen peroxide to induce vomiting
- Ice pack
- Pet first- aid booklet
- Roll bandages (Vet-Wrap) that stretch and cling
- Saline solution or eye lubricant
- Scissors
- Telephone numbers for:
  - your vet
  - an after-hours emergency vet hospital
- Tweezers

self-grooming (and the accumulation of a lot of hair in the intestine), the acquisition of stones, dirt, or gravel in the bowel, or even certain medication. Elderly intact males can have an enlarged prostate gland that presses on the colon, which may contribute to constipation.

Simple constipation can be corrected with a simple enema—but let the vet do it. It's easier, believe me. In some cases, stool softeners or other medication to increase the motility of the large intestines may be given. In the old days, mineral oil was used for this purpose, better and safer medications are available today.

You may also want to add fibre to your dog's diet, and your vet may suggest a prescription diet for this purpose. Or you can simply add tinned pumpkin, bran cereal, or even Metamucil.

Weims who strain frequently to poop and produce bloody or mucous-covered stools are probably not constipated; rather, they are likely suffering from a large bowel infection.

Diarrhoea

Diarrhoea does not just occur all by itself. It is a sign of disease, the result of parasites, or a sequel to scavenging rubbish—even a medication might be the cause. Whatever the cause, though, it's important to remember that diarrhoea is always more dangerous in puppies than in adult dogs. The dehydration that diarrhoea causes can lead to extreme weakness or even death in puppies. Most cases of diarrhoea resolve in a day or so without interference, but if the diarrhoea is accompanied by lethargy, abdominal pain, vomiting, or blood in the stool, take your Weim to a vet right away and bring a sample of the diarrhoea with you.

Learn how to perform the Heimlich manoeuvre on your dog in case of choking.

Drooling

Most Weimaraners are not natural droolers. If your previously dry-mouthed Weim starts to drool, there may be trouble. Drooling is often the result of a cracked tooth or gum infection, but it also could be a sign of poisoning or something lodged in the throat. Check your dog's mouth to see if you can spot the problem (such as a foreign object, like a wedged stick). If there's something stuck in the throat, try to remove it. If you can't see anything, call your vet.

Grass Seeds

These seeds can penetrate your Weimaraner's skin and imbed themselves in his eyes, paws, or nose. If you can readily see the seed in the skin, you can pull it out. However, the seed can imbed itself far up the nose or under the third eyelid, making the dog sneeze uncontrollably or paw at his head. His eye also may look infected. This happened to one of my dogs once, years ago. I noticed a red, swollen eye and showed it to my guests, who happened to be people-doctors. They looked and looked and saw nothing. So I took the dog to the vet, who removed the seed and said, "Tell your doctor friends to look under the third eye next time." I did, and they said blankly, "Third eyelid? Dogs have an extra eyelid?" They do indeed. *C'est la différence.*

Insect Stings and Bites

Bees, wasps, and hornets are not your dog's best friends. Most stings occur in hairless areas, but the thin-coated Weim is in danger all over. The face is a common site because—let's face it—it's perfectly possible that your nosy Weim has just stuck his nose in a hornet's nest.

While you can probably see the results within 20 minutes after an attack, watch your dog for at least another 12 hours for further reaction, as mild signs may get progressively worse. Usually, however, a sting produces a local inflammation that will subside in an hour or so. Multiple stings are more dangerous and more likely to produce an allergic reaction. Large swelling or difficulty breathing could signal a severe allergic reaction or anaphylactic shock. This is an emergency.

If the stinger remains in your dog (as from the sting of a honeybee), do not use tweezers to extract it. That may actually inject *more* venom into the dog because the entire venom-containing apparatus is attached to the stinger. Try scraping the stinger out with your credit card. Then, apply a paste of water and baking soda, ammonia, calamine lotion, or a commercial product (if you have one readily available) to the area to relieve the itching. Use an ice pack or cold compress to relieve swelling and pain. If the dog has been stung in the mouth, feed only soft foods for a while because eating may be painful.

Avoid Laxatives Designed for Humans

Never use constipation products designed for people on dogs without your vet's consent. Enemas and laxatives can be harmful to dogs if not made for them.

If You See Your Dog Straining

Difficulty urinating also can appear as straining. Straining to urinate is often an emergency situation, so if there is any question about your pet's ability to urinate, see the vet right away.

Frostbite and Hypothermia

Just because your Weim has fur doesn't mean that he can't get cold. He can and does. Weims are not Siberian Huskies!

Hypothermia has several stages. When first exposed to cold, the dog hairs undergo something called "pilo-erection," fluffing out to provide better insulation. If the body's core temperature gets lower, the dog will begin to shiver; shivering is just an involuntary reflex by the skeletal muscles. If things get even worse, the body will respond by vasoconstricting the peripheral tissues to keep the core organs warm. In other words, the body shuts down the surface veins to keep the warm blood where it is most needed—in the brain, heart, liver, and so on. The dog is making a choice between his toes and ears versus his heart and brain. Guess who wins? This is how frostbite occurs.

Signs of frostbite include bright red tissues followed by greying or black tissues. To administer first aid, put the affected areas (not the whole dog) into a bath of warm (not hot) water. Dry gently, but do not rub the tissues—you could damage them further. Wrap your dog in a blanket and seek veterinary care.

If true hypothermia has set in, the core body temperature will be below 99.5 °F (37.5°C). Keep your Weim warm in blankets, and put bottles of warm water around him. Keep checking his temperature until it's back to normal, 101°F (38.5°C). Seek veterinary care as soon as possible.

Heatstroke

Heatstroke is a fever brought about by excessive temperature outside. It is most dangerous when the humidity is high, because evaporative cooling is less effective then. When the core body temperature rises above 104°F (40°C), heatstroke is already doing its damage. After 106.7°F (41.5°C), your dog is in serious danger of death.

Unlike humans, dogs aren't tropical animals. Heatstroke can

Moving an Injured Dog

Always use a muzzle before moving an injured dog because even the best-tempered dog can bite when he is afraid or in pain. If you suspect a back or neck injury, put the dog on a board to prevent further injury. Otherwise, if your Weim is still a puppy, carrying him is the easiest method. To prevent him from kicking you, hold the front and rear legs as you walk. Keep the injured side of the animal against you. If your Weim is an adult, he's probably too heavy to carry easily. In that case, place him on a blanket. Have one person carry each end like a stretcher. Again, if you suspect back or neck injury, use a stiff board instead.

occur when they are left outside without shade or water, when they overexercise in hot, humid weather (a real danger with Weims), or of course when left in a car, even with the windows partially open. Older dogs, obese dogs, puppies, and animals with medical problems are most at risk.

Signs of heatstroke include:
- heavy, loud breathing
- a staggering gait
- bright red tongue or gums

To prevent heatstroke, feed your dog during the coolest times of the day—early morning and evening. Make sure that he has plenty of fresh, cool water.

If your dog gets heatstroke and is unconscious, apply CPR. (See pages 182-183.) If he is conscious, get him in the shade and hose him down or put him in the shower with cool (not cold) water, soaking his paws, belly, and ears really well. Put rubbing alcohol on the pads of the feet. When his temperature reaches 102.2°F (39°C), stop the cooling efforts. Keep taking his temperature every five minutes and head for the vet. Dogs can suffer consequences of heatstroke for days afterward.

Lumps and Bumps

Lumps and bumps are very common in Weimaraners, especially in geriatric pets. They may be nothing at all, or they may be a highly malignant form of cancer. Benign lumps include sebaceous cysts, hair follicle cysts, fatty tumours (lipomas, which usually occur on heavy dogs), folliculitis, warts, sebaceous hyperkeratosis, or epulis (nodular growths in the oral cavity). Malignancies include mast cell tumours, basal cell tumours, skin or lymph gland lymphomas, and melanomas.

Grass seeds can embed themselves in the eyes, paws, or nose.

Only your vet can diagnose your Weim's lump or bump. And she can tell nothing without testing, usually with a fine needle aspirate if the contents are largely fluid or through a biopsy if they are not. Until the lump is

diagnosed, it's not possible to properly treat it. It is better to be overly cautious than to ignore the problem. Don't let fear keep you from the vet—many lumps, even cancerous ones, are treatable if caught early.

The more observant you are, the better you can assist your vet in treating a lump. Be as prepared as you can to answer these questions:

- Is the lump painful, bleeding, itchy, or tender?
- Does it seem attached to the bone?
- Is there only one lump or multiple similar lumps?
- Is it growing in size?
- Is it soft or hard?
- How long has it been there and how has it changed?
- How old is the dog?
- Where is the lump?
- Is the dog exhibiting other "sick signs" such as vomiting?

Poisoning

The poet Robert Louis Stevenson once wrote that the world is "so full of a number of things / I am sure we should all be as happy as kings." Unfortunately for this optimistic line of thought, many of the things in the world are toxic.

However, toxins are not all equally toxic. The damage that is done depends not only on the nature of the poison but on how much was ingested and how long it stays in the body before treatment. If you are quick enough, you may be able to save your dog from any permanent harm. On the other hand, some substances are so deadly and fast acting that nothing you can do will save your dog.

Signs of poisoning vary with the substance, but common ones include difficulty breathing, sluggishness, loss of appetite, vomiting, stumbling or wobbling, and seizure. If your dog exhibits any of these and you suspect poisoning, take him to the vet along with a sample of urine, faeces, or vomitus, if possible. If you know what your dog has eaten, take along a sample of that as well.

Unless your Weim has devoured something corrosive or a petroleum-based product, inducing vomiting is helpful if the event occurred less than two hours previously. Only attempt this if your dog is conscious! You or your vet also can try to delay absorption by administering activated charcoal, which binds to the toxin and prevents further absorption. Some poisons, like ethylene glycol (antifreeze), lead, arsenic, anticoagulant rodenticides, and acetaminophen, have special antidotes that can be given. Even if there is no specific antidote, your vet can give supportive care, such as oxygen therapy, IV fluids, pain medication, sedatives, seizure control, and heat.

Acetaminophen

Tylenol and similar products can damage the liver and red blood cells. Signs of toxicity such as depression, abdominal pain, and vomiting occur within hours. The urine may be dark. If your dog has ingested acetaminophen, induce vomiting and get him to a vet right away.

Antifreeze

What's good for your car can kill your Weimaraner. The deadly ingredient in many antifreeze products is ethylene glycol. This substance is metabolised by the liver and travels through the kidneys, where it forms insoluble calcium oxalate crystals. They cause permanent damage to the kidney tissue, which can ultimately lead to kidney failure.

The first signs of antifreeze toxicity are depression and lethargy; many dogs appear intoxicated. Later signs include vomiting and renal failure, followed by death three or four days later. Your vet has a test kit to detect the presence of this poison in the body. The initial signs can last from one to six hours. Treatment for ethylene glycol toxicity may require extended hospitalization, and even then it is not

Don't let your Weim overexercise in hot, humid weather.

Making a Muzzle

You can manufacture a muzzle out of any handy suitable material, like tights, ties, twine, or a belt. Practice making one at home before an emergency so that you'll feel more confident. Tie a knot in the middle of the material, then make a large loop to slip over the dog's nose. (Stand to the side to be out of the way of a biter.) Tighten the loop quickly and twist the other two ends underneath the muzzle, then tie them behind the ears at the back of the head.

always successful. Newer kinds of antifreeze are on the market that use propylene glycol instead of ethylene glycol. This newer product is somewhat safer than the old kind—you can even find propylene glycol in toothpaste.

Chocolate

As much as they love it, chocolate is toxic to dogs (cats, too). It is full of fat, caffeine, and theobromine, which can stimulate the nervous system to a dangerous degree. The general rule is that the darker the chocolate, the more theobromine it contains. White chocolate, for example is so innocuous that your Weimaraner would probably need to eat 100 pounds (45.3 kg) of it before the theobromine affected him. (And believe me, after eating that much of anything, a dog gets sick.) So don't worry about white chocolate. Milk chocolate starts to get dangerous if your Weimaraner eats more than a around a kilogram of it. That's not too likely either, although it's certainly possible. Twelve ounces (340 g) of semi-sweet chocolate is dangerous to a Weim-sized dog, but only 4 ounces (113 g) of baking chocolate can induce signs of toxicity, including restlessness, hyperactivity, muscle twitching, increased urination, and excessive panting. The fat in the chocolate may cause diarrhoea and vomiting. None of this is pleasant, especially because you were keeping the chocolate for yourself—so lock up the chocolate! If your Weimaraner got into it, call your vet. Animals treated for chocolate toxicity usually recover within 24 to 48 hours.

Grapes and Raisins

In the past few years, it's been noted that ingesting large amounts (more than 9 ounces [255 g]) of grapes or raisins can be toxic to dogs, causing kidney failure. The precise toxic substance responsible has not yet been determined.

Plants

As a general precaution, it's best not to allow your Weimaraner to graze. Many plants contain toxins, and even those that don't are largely unsuitable for dogs. However, the four plants that seem to be eaten the most are:

- Azaleas: These landscape beauties contain toxins that can produce vomiting, drooling, diarrhoea, weakness, and central nervous system depression. Severe cases could lead to death from cardiovascular collapse.

- Lilies: For some reason, lilies are especially dangerous to cats, although they're not good for dogs, either. Consuming even small amounts can result in severe kidney damage.
- Oleander: Oleander, an ornamental, can cause severe irritation of the gastrointestinal tract, hypothermia, and severe cardiac problems.
- Sago Palm: Another popular ornamental, the sago palm can produce vomiting, diarrhoea, depression, seizures, liver failure, and even death. Both the leaves and the base of the plant appear to be toxic.

Rodenticides

The same stuff that kills mice and rats can kill your dog. The most common rodenticides used are anticoagulants, which block the clotting mechanisms in the blood and cause internal bleeding. If left untreated, the bleeding continues until the animal dies. Unfortunately, most rodenticides have a delayed onset; haemorrhage may not begin until three to five days after a dog eats the stuff. If you did not see your dog eat it, you might not know that anything is wrong until he exhibits typical signs, such as weakness, pale mucous membranes, rapid breathing, or haemorrhage. Even worse, some anticoagulants can produce effects lasting for up to three to four weeks. The classic therapy is a prescription of Vitamin K1, administered on a regular basis until the effects of the poison are gone. It is also critical to retest for bleeding problems after the therapy has ended. Obviously, the best way to avoid poisoning is not to use rodenticides.

Dangers lurk everywhere for curious puppies—check your garden is puppy proofed.

Tobacco

Strangely enough, some dogs chew or even swallow tobacco. But it's not good for them; in fact, nicotine is a deadly poison. The toxic dose for nicotine in pets is 20 to 100 mg, and a cigarette contains 9 to 30 mg of nicotine. The butt of the cigarette (the most likely part to be ingested by your Weim, who finds it on the ground) contains about 25 percent of the original amount of nicotine in the

If You Suspect Poison

Many poisons are slow acting. If you believe that your dog has eaten something toxic, get him to the vet even if he shows no signs of illness. If you think that your pet may have been poisoned, contact your local veterinarian.

cigarette. Signs of nicotine poisoning are tremors, vomiting, diarrhoea, and twitching or seizures. The dog's blood pressure also can rise dangerously high. If your dog exhibits any of these signs, take him to the vet.

Vomiting

Dogs are expert vomiters. As scavengers, their digestive systems are designed to gobble up anything lying around now and throw up the bad stuff later. They vomit easily and with aplomb. So if your dog vomits once or twice, then stops and acts normal, there is probably nothing to worry about. However, vomiting also can be a sign of many diseases of the stomach or intestines, or it can be secondary to conditions such as cancer, kidney failure, diabetes, intestinal obstruction, and infectious disease, especially if the vomiting is repeated or ineffectual.

Blood in the vomit is a serious sign. And if your dog exhibits other signs in addition to vomiting, such as diarrhoea, dehydration, loss of appetite, fever, pain, abdominal pain, or lethargy, it's definitely time to call the vet.

ALTERNATIVE THERAPIES

While traditional Western medicine is probably the best modality for treating many conditions, some chronic problems, especially pain, respond very well to less invasive alternative treatments. These include:

Acupuncture

Acupuncture uses fine needles at precise points on the dog's body to redirect and rebalance energy. Stimulation of these points results in physiological and biochemical changes that produce a healing effect..

Chiropractic

Chiropractic care is aimed at restoring the proper relationship between the spine and the rest of the nervous system to improve health. In chiropractic lingo, it works to correct "subluxations," or bones that are out of proper alignment. Misalignment can cause all kinds of painful symptoms, such as abnormal posture, odd position of the tail, loss of flexibility, behavioural changes like fear-biting, weakness, and lack of coordination.

Herbal Therapy

Many people use herbs to nutritionally support the healing process. In some cases, herbs may be curative

Homeopathy

Homeopathy uses highly diluted chemicals and herbs to stimulate the immune system. Homeopathy is derived from the Greek word *homoios*, which means "like" or "similar." It operates on the system of "like cures like." Homeopathic medicines (called "remedies") are prepared from pure, natural, animal, vegetable, or mineral substances listed in the European Pharmacopoeia. They are created in modern labs by a process of serial dilution and succussion (repeated shaking). During this process, the medicines are diluted with water and alcohol from ten times to millions of times. The medicines come in pill or liquid form and are usually administered orally. These medicines are inexpensive, have no unwanted side effects, and are safe for newborns, oldsters, and pregnant or lactating dogs. However, it is only fair to say that the efficacy of homeopathic therapy has not been substantiated by scientific studies.

Keep your Weim safely on a lead when you are out and about.

Magnetic Therapy

In magnetic therapy, magnets are placed under the dog's bed to balance the energy flow.

Massage

Massage provides both physical and mental benefits beyond the well-known relaxing of tight muscles. It also improves flexibility, aids the flow of blood, nutrients, and oxygen, promotes a healthy coat, and relaxes the dog. Just as important, by accustoming your dog to a loving touch, it helps to build a bond between you. There are some caveats, however. Never massage a dog who is in shock or who has a fever— or any dog who has an undiagnosed illness. And don't massage places with infections, lumps, or wounds. If your dog has cancer, check with your vet about the advisability of massaging him. If your dog is closing his eyes and relaxing during the procedures (and doesn't try to get away), you know that he is enjoying the attentive touching.

Massage can be given twice a week. If you can teach your Weim to give *you* a massage, that's even better. You deserve one.

Tellington TTouch

One variety of massage is called the Tellington TTouch massage. It uses a combination of different lifts, movement exercises, and touches to activate the nervous system to help correct behaviour problems (such as aggression and chewing), improve quality of life for ageing pets, and can even help with carsickness.

Trigger-point Therapy

Trigger-point therapy is a treatment that uses pressure on specific trigger points on muscles to relieve nerve inflammation.

CARING FOR THE SENIOR WEIMARANER

Your old friend is more likely to develop aches and pains as he ages; he is also more prone to cancer, diabetes, and other diseases. The best offence is a good defence. Visit your veterinarian frequently—at least once every six months. It's also important to groom your dog often because older dogs often will do less self-care than they did when younger. Because his skin isn't as elastic as it used to be, don't scrape! Take note of any hair loss or unusual lumps or bumps. Include a daily tooth brushing session, which helps to prevent gum disease and tooth loss. An increase in "dog breath" can signal trouble. Clip his nails, too. Good grooming also means the use of flea and tick prevention. Older dogs also appreciate a daily massage, especially if they're not able to exercise.

Do keep your older dog as mentally and physically active as possible. Exercise helps to maintain muscle tone, cardiac strength, and good digestion. Moderate, regular exercise will add years to your Weim's active life.

Older dogs need smaller, more frequent meals with high-quality protein. In fact, older dogs need about 50 percent more protein than their young adult counterparts. Choose a food especially designed for seniors, and keep tabs on his weight. Make sure that he always has ready access to fresh, cool water.

As your dog ages, he may need more potty breaks; try to accommodate him. Neither his digestion nor bladder and bowel control is what it once was.

A regular schedule is much appreciated for both physical and mental reasons. Older dogs can't cope with stress as well as younger ones, and a regular schedule makes them feel more secure.

Make sure that your older dog has a comfortable, draft-free bed, and don't relegate him to the back garden. He needs to be a real part of the family now more than ever.

THE LAST GOODBYE

The decision to let your Weim go is difficult, even in the best of circumstances. To help you decide when the time has come, devise a list of criteria, such as:

- Is my Weim still eating?
- Is my Weim in pain?
- Does my Weim still enjoy some activities?

If the answers to these questions suggest that the end is near, it may be time to call your vet to make arrangements.

An equally difficult decision for many is whether to be present at the end. You will probably be torn between not wanting to leave your dog alone at this hard time and the fear that you cannot stand to be present. This is a personal decision that only you can make. Your veterinarian may be able to help you decide. Your Weim will understand either way.

As is the way of all life, eventually your beloved Weim will return to the mists and the mystery that gave him birth. You are left with heartache for the beloved friend who is gone. Grief is natural and personal. Your grief belongs to you and to those who loved your dog. It does not have to follow "steps" or "stages" or anything like that. It is an individual matter.

But there is also, hidden deep in your heart, a faint stirring of hope. The universe is more wonderful than we know, and if any breed can plumb its misty depths and return to us in spirit or even in the flesh, it is the wonderfully named Grey Ghost. Such things are not impossible.

While you are waiting, the memories of this magnificent dog will always be yours: tough and tender, sweet and strong. A slash of silver splitting the grey dawn: gossamer and steel.

Extra TLC

Your Veteran Weim needs extra love and care to help him through his senior years. Beware of potential aches and pains that didn't show before. Make sure he is eating right and getting enough exercise—and rest!

You want him to be comfortable as he lives out his days.

ASSOCIATIONS AND ORGANISATIONS

Breed Clubs

American Kennel Club (AKC)
5580 Centerview Drive
Raleigh, NC 27606
Telephone: (919) 233-9767
Fax: (919) 233-3627
E-mail: info@akc.org
www.akc.org

Canadian Kennel Club (CKC)
89 Skyway Avenue, Suite 100
Etobicoke, Ontario M9W 6R4
Telephone: (416) 675-5511
Fax: (416) 675-6506
E-mail: information@ckc.ca
www.cka.ca

Federation Cynologique Internationale (FCI)
Secretariat General de la FCI
Place Albert 1er, 13
B – 6530 Thuin
Belqique
www.fci.be

The Kennel Club
1 Clarges Street
London
W1J 8AB
Telephone: 0870 606 6750
Fax: 0207 518 1058
www.the-kennel-club.org.uk

United Kennel Club (UKC)
100 E. Kilgore Road
Kalamazoo, MI 49002-5584
Telephone: (269) 343-9020
Fax: (269) 343-7037
E-mail: pbickell@ukcdogs.com
www.ukcdogs.com

Weimaraner Club of Great Britain
www.weimaranerclubof
greatbritain.org.uk

The North of England Weimaraner Society (N.E.W.S.)
www.norther-weimaraner.org.uk

Weimaraner Club of Scotland
www.weimaraner-scotland.com

The Weimaraner Association
www.weimaraner-association.org.uk

Rescue Organisations and Animal Welfare Groups

Royal Society for the Prevention of Cruelty to Animals (RSPCA)
Telephone: 0870 3335 999
Fax: 0870 7530 284
www.rspca.org.uk

British Veterinary Association Animal sWelfare Foundation
7 Mansfield Street
London W1G 9NQ
Telephone: 0207 436 2970
Email: bva-awf@bva.co.uk
www.bva-awf.org.uk

Scottish Society for the Prevention of Cruelty to Animals (SSPCA)
Braehead Mains, 603 Queensferry Road
Edinburgh EH4 6EA
Telephone: 0131 339 4777
Email: enquiries@scottishspca.org
www.scottishspca.org

Dogs Trust
17 Wakley Street
London
EC1V 7RQ
Telephone: 0207 837 0006
www.dogstrust.org.uk

Weimaraner Rescue
www.weimaraner-rescue.org.uk

The Independent Weimaraner Rescue & Rehoming Service
www.champdogs.co.uk

Sports

Canine Freestyle Federation, Inc.
Membership Secretary:
Brandy Clymire
E-mail: CFFmemberinfo@aol.com
www.canine-freestyle.org

International Agility Link (IAL)
Global Administrator: Steve Drinkwater
E-mail: yunde@powerup.au
www.agilityclick.com/~ial

Therapy
Pets As Therapy
3a Grange Farm Cottages
Wycombe Road
Saunderton
Princes Risborough
Bucks
HP27 9NS

Training & Behaviour
Association of Pet Dog Trainers (APDT)
PO Box 17
Kampsford GL7 4W7
Telephone: 01285 810 811

Association of Pet Behaviour Counsellors
PO Box 46
Worcester WR8 9YS
Telephone: 01386 750743
Email:: info@apbc.org.uk
www.apbc.org.uk

British Institute of Professional Dog Trainers
www.bipdt.net

Veterinary and Health Resources
British Veterinary Association (BVA)
7 Mansfield Street
London, England
W1G 9NQ
Telephone: 020 7636 6541
E-mail: bvahq@bva.co.uk
www.bva.co.uk

British Veterinary Hopitals Association (BHVA)
Station Bungalow
Main Road, Stockfield
Northumberland NE43 7HJ
Telephone: 07966 901619
Email: office@bvha.org.uk
www.BVHA.org.uk

Royal College of Veterinary Surgeons (RCVS)
Belgravia House
62-64 Horseferry Road
London SW1P 2AF
Telephone: 0207 222 2001
Email: admin@rcvs.org.uk
www.rcvs.org.uk

Association of Chartered Physiotherapists Specialising in Animal Therapy (ACPAT)
52 Littleham Road
Exmouth, Devon EX8 2QJ
Telephone: 01395 270648
Email: bexsharples@hotmail.com
www.acpat.org.uk

Association of British Veterinary Acupuncturists (ABVA)
66A Easthorpe, Southwell
Nottinghamshire NG25 0HZ
Email: jonnyboyvet@hotmail.com
www.abva.co.uk

Pet Sitters
National Association of Registered Petsitters
www.dogsit.com

UK Petsitters
www.ukpetsitter.com

Dog Services UK
www.dogservices.co.uk

PUBLICATIONS

BOOKS

Dominique De Vito
Training Your Dog
Interpet Publishing, 2007

Nester, Mary Ann
Agility Dog Training
Interpet Publishing, 2007

O'Neill
What Dog?
Interpet Publishing, 2006

Harvey, Su
Good Pup, Good Dog
Interpet Publishing, 2007

Evans, J M
What If My Dog?
Interpet Publishing, 2005

Tennant, Colin
Mini Encyclopedia of Dog Training & Behaviour
Interpet Publishing, 2006

Barnes, Julia
Living With A Rescued Dog
Interpet Publishing, 2004

Evans, J M & White, Kay
Doglopaedia
Ringpress Books, 1998

Evans, J M
Book of The Bitch
Ringpress Books, 1998

Magazines

Dogs Monthly
Ascot House
High Street, Ascot,
Berkshire SL5 7JG
Telephone: 0870 730 8433
E-mail: admin@rtc-associates.freeserve.co.uk
www.corsini.co.uk/dogsmonthly

Dog World Ltd
Somerfield House
Wotton Road, Ashford
Kent TN23 6LW
Telephone: 01233 621 877

Dogs Today
Town Mill, Bagshot Road
Chobham
Surrey GU24 8BZ
Telephone: 01276 858880
Email: enquiries@dogstodaymagazine.co.uk
www.dogstodaymagazine.co.uk

Kennel Gazette
Kennel Club
1 Clarges Street
London W1J 8AB
Telehone: 0870 606 6750
www.thekennelclub.co.uk

K9 Magazine
21 High Street
Warsop
Nottinghamshire NG20 0AA
Telephone: 0870 011 4114
Email: mail@k9magazine.com
www.k9magazine.com

Our Dogs
Our Dogs Publishing
5 Oxford Road
Station Approach
Manchester
M60 1SX
www.ourdogs.co.uk

Your Dog
Roebuck House
33 Broad Street
Stamford
Lincolnshire PE9 1RB
Telephone: 01780 766199

INDEX

ACKNOWLEDGMENTS

To all my great friends at TFH for their kindness and patience!

DEDICATION

To all my friends at Cumberland Valley Animal Clinic.

ABOUT THE AUTHOR

In her spare time (away from her animals), Diane Morgan is an assistant professor of philosophy and religion at Wilson College, Chambersburg, PA. She has authored numerous books on canine care and nutrition and has also written many breed books, horse books, and books on Eastern philosophy and religion. She is an avid gardener (and writes about that, too). Diane lives in Williamsport, Maryland with several dogs, two cats, some fish, and a couple of humans.

PHOTO CREDITS